I'M RICH
YOU'RE POOR

I'M RICH
YOU'RE POOR

How to give social media a reality check

SHABAZ ALI

with Oscar Millar

Shabaz is a thoughtful yet funny writer, and I've never been so proud to be a povvo! I really enjoyed this entertaining – and sometimes unexpected! – read.

LalalaLetMeExplain

Hilarious, articulate, honest and frank, Shabaz gets to the point with his quick-witted mockery of the modern-day social media trends and people. His writing mirrors what we see of his personality online and we couldn't stop reading. Obsessed!

Lauren and Rachel Finch (fellow Blackburnians!)

This book is 'vicked!' Silly, funny, yet very insightful.

Tez Ilyas

Hilarious and thought provoking!

Davina McCall

Shabaz Ali pokes at those of us who use social media as a facade. In a world where many of us are feeling fatigued from overly polished content, Shabaz's sharp commentary, delivered with wit and in a fuzzy onesie, puts these topics into clearer context.

Adam Mosseri, Head of Instagram

Shabaz's book is a much-needed reality check for the digital population. His wisdom, honesty and understanding of the human experience reminds us what truly matters in life and why it's vital that we are able to differentiate between our realities and the digital noise on our screen. With his encouragement to pause, reflect and reconnect with the tangible aspects of our existence, he reminds us that while technology has an unavoidable (and often necessary) place in our lives, it should never replace the genuine connections and experiences that ground us.

Abby Parker @abbysbooks

Smart, witty and refreshing – had me laughing out loud one second and thinking deeply the next.

Katie Piper OBE

A brilliantly witty, always hilarious and unapologetically cutting take on everything that is wrong with social media. I've never loved Quavers so much!

Dr Ranj

As a fellow povvo, I love Shabaz and this book because it is informative, hilarious and relatable.

Fats Timbo

I love this book as much as I love my fridge full of assorted flavour ice! Will make you fall in love with social media again.

Laura Whitmore

To my povvo gang who have been there since the beginning.
This one is for you.

Editorial Director Elizabeth Neep
Project Editor Izzy Holton
Senior Production Editor Tony Phipps
Senior Production Controller Samantha Cross
Art Director Maxine Pedliham
Publishing Director Katie Cowan

Cover photographs by Mark Harrison

First published in Great Britain in 2024 by
Dorling Kindersley Limited
DK, One Embassy Gardens, 8 Viaduct Gardens,
London, SW11 7BW

The authorised representative in the EEA is
Dorling Kindersley Verlag GmbH. Arnulfstr. 124,
80636 Munich, Germany

A CIP catalogue record for this book
is available from the British Library.
ISBN: 978-0-2416-8932-5
Printed and bound in the United Kingdom

www.dk.com

MIX
Paper | Supporting
responsible forestry
FSC™ C018179

This book was made with Forest
Stewardship Council™ certified
paper – one small step in DK's
commitment to a sustainable future.
Learn more at
www.dk.com/uk/information/sustainability

CONTENTS

CONTENTS

BEG YOUR PARD
ROUND BALLY IC
RICH, YOU'RE PO
SPOKEN LIKE A
POVVO, BECAUS
NOT AN ANIMAL
WHY?, BECAUSE
YOU'RE A POVVO
WHAT ON GOD'S
EARTH, ON TODA
PISODE OF..., RO
SISTER SHERRIE
HAVE A DAY OFF
GASP, STOP IT I

INTRODUCTION

Does anybody really read the introduction in a book? Well, I think we know the answer to that question, don't we?

You do. Because you want to get your money's worth, you beautiful povvo.[1]

Like me, you'll read the contents page and the acknowledgements if it'll stretch out your pound. You'll stay in your cinema seat for *all* the credits, until you've found out who the 'Best boy' or 'First grip' was, and even who did the Korean subtitles. I can picture how you shrugged off the tutting from Row 6 when you opened your own Tupperware of popcorn.[2] And your sweets from home. And the loudest can of Diet Coke on God's green earth. You may or may not have borrowed a pair of your mum's bifocals to see if it made the 2D screening of *Avatar* feel 3D.

Speaking from experience, it never does, but when your wallet is in one dimension, these decisions are made for us.

And that can make us feel powerless. It can make us feel odd – not being able to do and buy the things that we are told we should. We are made to think that the 3D screening or the cinema popcorn or the Hermès bag (yes, I've jumped a few levels there, but you know what I mean) are the normal options. That if you can't have them, then you are somehow the odd one out. I don't buy it (to be fair, I don't buy a lot of things). Because if you can't have the Hermès/popcorn bag, then you are not odd, you are normal. You are one of many, and that is special.

Because being one of the ordinary people used to be a good thing. You were part of a community that shared in its

---

[1] For anyone who is new here, 'povvo' is used in the north of England to mean a poor person. I have repurposed it to mean anyone who isn't rich enough to show off about it professionally on Instagram.

[2] With the effortless ease of someone who has been doing it for 10 years.

losses and victories, and felt better for it. We celebrated things like weddings and babies and Christmas or Eid, not handbags. We shared beautiful moments in normal lives and we felt happy. So what went wrong? What happened that made us believe we all had to be special, beautiful and rich? That we had to have more and be more and pretend that the two were connected. To film it all.

I think we all know. Step one was consumerism and the second was social media, and when the two things met, they created a monster.

I have lived with that monster and I'm sure you have too. It's not really envy or jealousy, even if it looks like it. It's not a green-eyed monster, it's red-eyed, from scrolling through videos of people opening enough boxes of trainers to keep a millipede in Yeezys for life. It's red-eyed from silently crying into a tub of knock-off Jen&Berries[3] as another fitness influencer or beauty queen 'Just Wakes Up Like This'. It's red-eyed, because it's three in the blooming morning and, unlike the person making a video about their perfect daily routine, you have to be up at 6:30 for work. The feeling is not jealousy – it is self-loathing, because the Internet has made us hate ourselves.

It has made us feel poorer, uglier and less capable than we are and, in my case, it has often *actually* made me poorer, uglier and less capable than I am (due to online shopping, Jen&Berries and the mind-numbing powers of scrolling). Yes, my dear povvo, social media has birthed a monster that is sucking out the joy from us all, and I have come to slay it with a little thing called community (*strums opening chords of kumbaya – looks smug*).

Because if I have learnt one thing from relentlessly

---

3 Not a real brand. Should be.

mocking the performatively perfect online, it is not the things they have or the supposed jealousy they create that leave us all worse off – it's the isolation. It's not the performative perfection or even social media itself that is the problem, it is the loneliness of feeling like you are the only imperfect one. When you have community on the Internet, when you share and laugh, though – that aspect falls away. It's a healthier place because it is a shared one. I call that place '*anti*social media'. It is a space where we can all roll around in the dirt with our left-over curry in repurposed margarine tubs and generally have a laugh. Because staring at rich people is not the problem; staring at rich and beautiful people and believing that you are the only poor or ugly one at the party really is.

I think that's why the comments sections on my pages are genuinely joyful places, and it's why I have leant on them for so much of the content in this book. They are like one of those medieval festivals where all the ploughmen and serving wenches get together and have a bawdy knees-up.[4] It's a place where we admit that being a povvo takes skill, and that being a povvo is great because we are the only ones who seem to actually have any fun. Because, I don't know if anyone's noticed, but the lives of plastic people we stare at online do *not* look fun. They holiday in Dubai and alphabetise their cosmetics, their most meaningful relationships are with customer service assistants (who hate them) and they seem to drink all the time but never act drunk. It's actually like Dante created a circle of hell for the 2020s. Or Tantalus made

---

[4] This is actually more accurate than I first realised. Apparently, the original 'Feast or Festival of Fools' was when power was turned upside down and the povvos got together and made fun of the usual solemn duties of those in charge, which is basically what we are doing with social media icons now. I'm feeling real solidarity with my 12th-century spirit wench.

a TikTok. With George Orwell doing the 1984-style hashtags:

#HolidayIsWork

#FriendshipIsBought

#MessyNightsArePhotoOps

When your job is having a fun life, you end up turning all the fun in your life into hard work.

Imagine someone told you today that your new life was as a wealth influencer. Would you be happy? You might be glad to work less, and be able to buy a few nice things. Maybe you'd like a holiday. But would you really like all the things you own to become the basis of your personality? Your career? Your life?

I know you wouldn't, and neither would I. Though I have to admit that I wouldn't say no to a bit more money. I would like to be able to buy a few more things, and I would like to feel more attractive. I definitely do not think that being pretty or buying things is inherently bad. I just think showing off about it is, and I think the ways people show off on the Internet are completely hilarious. So more power to the show-offs. As long as we can keep laughing, they can keep twirling in pumpkin fields and telling me how to pronounce Lous Vuitton correctly.

I felt I had to say that – mainly because I don't wanna seem entirely poisonous, but also because, if I hadn't, I would be making a problem for myself. If people think I just fundamentally loathe anyone who is rich, beautiful or happy, then

" "

I definitely do not think that being pretty or buying things is inherently bad. I just think showing off about it is, and I think the ways people show off on the Internet are completely hilarious.

I'm never allowed to be any of those things. I don't want to be poor, alone and unhappy for my whole life, but if my whole identity (and credibility) is tied to being the 'Poor Alone Guy', then I have a serious issue. I'd like to be richer, I'd like to have a healthy, happy relationship and I would love to have a vaguely functional routine, but if I start telling you about how great it is, then put on your onesie and light up the torches, there's a Shabaz to be mocked.

I'm glad I've had this chance to manage expectations. As a grown man who appears almost exclusively in the public eye wearing a Harry Potter onesie, I have had to learn about doing this the hard way. People are surprised when I am *not* wearing a dirty onesie to the shops, to work. They are surprised that I am not lying down when they see me, even in places where lying down is really not a practical choice (the road or public toilets). People seem to confuse my social media content with my reality, and I think a similar confusion is at the heart of our problems with wealth/beauty/happiness influencers.

We mistakenly assume influencers are using social media for the same reason that most of us are – to show people nice snippets of our lives (albeit filtered, modified, idealised ones) – whereas, in reality, they are running a business. They are making their own little reality series that they cast and produce and happen to broadcast on a platform designed for showcasing real people's lives. This understandably confuses people. Broadcasting is for TV, fiction is for books and film crews are for movies, not social media. So when we go on social media, we forget that we are watching people using a film crew to broadcast their fictional life. They are just making really bad reality TV shows. When you see them that way, they are far more entertaining and far less toxic. The Real Housewives of TikTok. The Only Way is Insta. Selling Sunsets (and also a 10-week self-actualisation and alignment course).

To counter this problem, I think we all just need to start posting more really rubbish stuff on the Internet. I mean *really* rubbish, though, not just #nomakeupselfies or 'look how cute/ ugly my dog is'. I'm talking about whatever your aunties and uncles put on their Facebook page but to the power of 10. Photos of your kitchen floor when the budget bin bag splits. Videos of the meals you don't want people to see (Shabaz's cheese 'n' bean pasta bake anyone?). Pictures from that one night on your holiday when you and your boyfriend got drunk and shouted at each other in an alleyway because he just DOESN'T HAVE A PASSION FOR COUPLES PHOTOS.[5]

I don't know if that would stop people expecting me to wear a onesie all the time, but it would at least return a sense of reality to proceedings.

It would also be a very British thing to do because, in my home country of the UK, the good things about your life are not to be shared, they are to be hidden. My best guess is that this is a result of our history of class and colonialism (like all the good things). Rich people in the UK have known for a long time that they can only be so rich on the back of generational wealth (AKA keeping things from local povvos) or colonialism (AKA taking things from distant povvos) so they keep quiet about it. The model British citizen is one of those bumbling aristocrats in a Channel 4 doc whose family may have owned half of Bengal but who wears biscuit-encrusted jumpers. On camera they're talking about how they need emergency loans from the National Trust to save their home, but under the table they're texting a car dealer about their next Lamborghini and rubbing more biscuits into their jumper in the hope that it will make us forget about the Koh-i-

---

5 Based on a true story.

noor.[6] That's good honest British dishonesty. We should put them on Instagram. It's the patriotic thing to do.

In the USA, it feels to me like it's the opposite: if things are great, then it is probably because you are, too, and people should know about it and learn from it. The Americans have a dream and centuries of legally entrenched oppression (slavery and racial segregation to name but two), which means that they've never had to hide their wealth. They know that what they've got they have earnt and, even if they actually haven't earnt it, they've got a police force which will stop anyone who is not rich or white from taking it back. So take them off Instagram. It's the patriotic thing to do.

If we can find the middle ground between the UK and US outlooks, then maybe the Internet can be a guiding light towards equality. (Can you imagine that?) If we can find a consensus, by becoming more honest than Brits about what we have and less shameless than Americans, then maybe we can actually approach the issue of inequality without being so damn confused.

That is what this book is. It is the end of inequality.

OK, maybe not. It is an attempt to bring the Internet's performative perfection down to size, and to big-up the beauty of normal people's lives. My hope is that each chapter will make you think a bit about the ridiculousness of how simple things are presented online (clothes, food, love) and the excellence of how the rest of us actually live. It will remind you that you are doing just fine, and maybe give you some pointers from the povvo hive mind about how to do just fine, finer. It will confirm that, although it looks nice to live in an ivory tower, it is much more fun to be part of the baying mob surrounding it.

----

[6] We still want it, Charles.' This is your moment. Give the diamond in the Queen Mother's Crown back or I'll tell everyone that Duchy Originals bananas don't really come from Cornwall (I jest…).

BEG YOUR PARL
ROUND BALLY IO
RICH, YOU'RE PO
SPOKEN LIKE A
POVVO, BECAUS
NOT AN ANIMAL
WHY?, BECAUSE
YOU'RE A POVVO
WHAT ON GOD'S
EARTH, ON TODA
EPISODE OF..., RO
SISTER SHERRIE
HAVE A DAY OFF
GASP, STOP IT

FOOD

ROY'S SISTER, SHEREE

Nothing really defines us like what we eat and how we eat it. In terms of health, this is obvious – our food can be the fine line between being sick and being healthy – but in terms of our identity, it is far more complex. A single meal can express my beliefs (vegetarian), culture (Lancashire/Pakistani) and class (working), which makes it a unique expression of both community and individuality. Food can bring us together and it can drive us apart. It's why we say, 'You are what you eat.'

Which, I think, makes me a Quaver.[1]

I mean, I was always salty and cheap, like this beloved British snack, but I can only assume that the Quavers made me more so. While I am uncomfortable with the fact that this might make me some sort of Quaver cannibal (Quannibal), coming to an understanding of my shared existence with a curly potato snack has definitely helped me to love myself more, because *to love oneself as one does crisps is the start of a beautiful relationship.*[2] This has been a blessing at a difficult time for me, as I have received the frightening diagnosis that I may, in fact, be a social media influencer. I can only assume that this has happened because I spent so much time having Instagrammers for breakfast and TikTokers on toast and, well, you are what you eat.

The fear that I might become an Instagram food person has grown with each passing day. I worry that if I laugh at enough eaters of high-priced strawberries, I may become one, too, and it has taken every ounce of Quaver within me to deal with the doubt. Will my heart be replaced by an ice

---

[1] Lol at you worrying that this book was going to be super serious for a second there.
[2] I think it was Oscar Wilde who said something like that.

cube of the same shape? Why am I tempted to video my morning routine? Maybe my life would be better if I just decanted my food into clear packaging?

But I have not given in. I have stayed strong. I will not be decanted.

So I would like to thank the Quavers for giving me strength but, most importantly, I would like to thank you, povvos. Every time I scrolled through videos of gold-plated steaks and worried that they would consume me, I had a comment section full of normal people discussing the beauty of the '10-second rule' and reminding me that gold probably tastes bad. When I almost got drawn in by a lemon-flavoured ice cube, someone mentioned storing curry in empty margarine tubs and I snapped out of my revelry. Someone compared caviar on toast to Findus Crispy Pancakes.[3] The strength I found in community and the joy of spilling the povvo tea was the only thing that saved me from losing myself. So, thank you, this book is dedicated to you, which it darn well should be, because a lot of it is also nicked from you as well. The stories and povvo hacks that are shared in this book come from the suggestions you have offered on my social media pages, and I would never have thought to write it if I hadn't had a pound shop hive mind buzzing around me. I'll thank you now and celebrate you later, because, before we discuss how you povvos are the solution to all the nonsense about food on the Internet, first I think we need to discuss the problem. The elephant in the room.

Many of you will probably be thinking, *Who's got an elephant in their room?* These rich people have gone too far!,

---

[3] These are actually nothing like caviar, toast or even pancakes. Sort of like a frozen, deep-fried calzone for the working class. The 'new' ones are made by Birds Eye.

but in this case I'm not using the phrase literally.[4] I'm referring to how social media is messing with our brains when it comes to food, and how food is just too important to get 'grammed, for all of the reasons we discussed at the start of the chapter. Food is not a hobby, it's not holidays and it's not designer leisurewear for pugs – it is basically life itself and therefore too important to get distorted by Internet thirst merchants. Have you ever wondered why conversations about food have, historically, been led by mums, religious leaders and then scientists (in that order)? Because these are important people (depending on your tastes) saying important things about an important subject. They are the ones we turn to. So I will not stand by as we trade 10,000 years of parental wisdom, 10,000 pages of Scripture and 10,000 academic articles from dieticians for 10-second videos of trust-fund babies eating $10 strawberries. We are what we eat and we need a reality check on who is serving us our identity.

So that is what this chapter – and, by extension, this book – aims to do. I want to take a step away from social media to look at what is *actually* going on there and to celebrate what is actually going on for the rest of us. To talk about the abnormality that has been normalised on the Internet, and then celebrate the reality of most people's relationship with food. I want to be

I want to take a step away from social media to look at what is actually going on there and to celebrate what is actually going on for the rest of us.

---

[4] An Instagram video entitled 'My Chic Elephant Kitchen' will be released tomorrow.

one part mum, one part religious (cult?) leader and one part social scientist[5] (qualifications pending) and provide a bit of perspective, which may fill in a tiny corner of the gaping lack of perspective that is our collective use of social media.

So, as we've already mentioned them, why don't we start with the high-priced strawberries?

Yes, there are $10 strawberries (allegedly, there are even more expensive ones but to keep our discussions on the right side of ridiculousness – OK, marginally less ridiculous – let's go with $10). Single berries. $10. That is either a disgrace or an amazing thing, depending on how you look at it. On the 'that's amazing' side of the room, we have influencers and the small subsection of the farming community who have managed to pull off this incredible coup. Looking at their side of the debate hall, I have to say, they make for an odd group. Some of them are wearing yoga pants and are videoing themselves doing peace signs beside a bunch of farmers, because farmers are *actually* 'Low-Key Chic'. The farmers seem confused, but you can see that most of them know this is a necessary evil. They are the ones selling the high-priced strawberries so, for them, these influencers are a blessing. They smile for the selfies that the Instagrammers take. One of them, a 65-year-old man with 17 generations of strawberry cultivation lineage behind him, wonders why the picture on the screen makes him look like an animated cat. He asks what his ancestors would think. Then he remembers. They would think, *Blooming well done! You sold those strawberries for $10 each. You are the best*

---

[5] I actually did a degree in forensic pathology, which is wild, I know. I feel it has served me well in my later career, though, as there are a lot of people saying 'I'm ded', which is pretty much the starting point for any forensic examination.

farmer. The farmer thinks, *Thank you*, his little animated cat eyes welling up as he looks to the sky.

Or maybe not, but you get what I mean. It is a strange marriage of the urban and rural, traditional and modern, practical and digital, that is going on between the luxury fruit producers and social media influencers. But it seems to work, so who am I to criticise the strawberry farmer and the 19-year-old millionaire for finding a way to support each other? Well, I'm Shabaz, and that's literally what I do, so here it goes.

The $10 strawberry is an abomination. It is a symbol of almost total societal, sensory and aesthetic decline. The $10 strawberry is not $10 because it tastes like a $10 strawberry, it is $10 because it looks like one. Very big and very red. Its bigness and redness is such that it looks like an emoji,[6] closer to the idea of a strawberry than an actual fruit, which may be why no one seems to wash them when they make videos unboxing and eating them. One of my followers mentioned that really big strawberries are less likely to be delicious than normal ones, as they have to up the water content to make them so bulbous. I hope that is true, because it forms the basis of my metaphor for the $10 strawberry as a symbol of much of Instagram's bloated falsity. The substance of strawberries has been substituted with water in the name of style, sacrificing sweetness and authenticity in the name of online visibility, and ending up worse for it. Which, if I say so myself, works just fine as a metaphor.

I think these superfruits needed the superficiality of the Internet to rise to where they are today. Social media works for boutique berries because, so often, style is prioritised

---

[6] Emojiberries could actually be a thing. Like a new superfruit. Goji berries with expressions.

over substance but also because exclusivity is a valuable commodity. Whereas once, having an exclusive fruit meant that you just had an exclusive fruit, and conversations about it could go something like:

'Hey, look at this.'

'What is it?'

'Look.'

'It's a fruit bowl.'

'Yeah, but look at the *fruit*!'

'Strawberries.'

'Yeah, but what *kind* of strawberries?'

'Big ones.'

'Yeah, tenner each.'

'Oh.'

Owning something that other people don't is actually an asset on social media because you can show it to everyone who doesn't have one at the same time. In a one-to-one setting, it is incredibly awkward to point out something you have that the other person doesn't, but on the Internet, it's a great and lucrative thing to do. This means that exclusivity is a commodity – it's an actual feature of a thing – when, in reality, exclusivity is the literal opposite of a feature. It is the absence of there being enough of something. From a farming perspective, it should be a clear failure but, thanks to influencers, our farmer can do his ancestors proud and sell one-hundredth of the strawberries they used to for a thousand times the price.

So where does our sympathy lie in this situation? For me, it's with the fruit. Fruit is used to being the thing that we are told to grow more of, have more of, eat more of (five a day, six a day, be ENTIRELY plant-based) and now it is getting dragged up into the ivory tower and being served as a single strawberry in a box. That is a lonely existence. Boxed into exclusivity. Becoming so beautiful that they live more to be looked at than enjoyed. They actually have more in common with the Instagrammers who eat them than I first realised.

I don't know how to feel about fruit as a status symbol versus your traditional show-off foods. On the one hand, growing beautiful fruit sort of makes sense: it's natural and healthy and people have been doing it for thousands of years. On the other hand, it somehow feels even more offensive than your caviars, gold-steaks and champagnes because, like money itself, those don't exactly grow on trees, whereas fruit does. I'm gonna check myself before I wreck myself,[7] though, by acknowledging that the whole expensive fruit thing came from Japan first and, apparently, they're traditionally given as special gifts. I am cool with that version of uber-fruit, and if it makes me a hypocrite so be it, but I feel like, in that case, people take the fruits of their labour and labour over their fruits to make someone else happy. It is the opposite of unboxing berries to get followers – which is a sentence that could only make sense in the 2020s, an ancient forest-dwelling community or a video game.

While I'm not sure we live in an ancient forest-dwelling community, I do think that a lot of what people do on the Internet has the feel of a video game. I have heard it said that Twitter (sorry, X) is a MMORPG (massive multiplayer online role-playing game) in which you gain XP by generating outrage (credit to Charlie Brooker and, later, Blindboy for developing this idea). In social media, I think it is about levelling up your avatar by means of extreme displays of joy,

----

[7] I just looked it up. The first person to say 'check yourself before you wreck yourself' was Ice Cube and, given we are discussing rich people's food habits, that must be a sign the universe is with us.

wealth or beauty.[8] Fruit works well for these as it allows you to display all three – joy (*Mmm... delicious*), wealth (mango = $100) *and* beauty (because the fruit is lovely and healthy and you are too), whereas most foods only level up your online avatar in one or two of these three dimensions. Take caviar, for example. There are loads of videos of people opening jars and eating caviar. That is all about the wealth, because, I'm sorry, there cannot be much joy in spooning black fish eggs on to a cracker, and, as for beauty, well, it's black fish eggs on a cracker.

Gold-plated steaks are also more about wealth than joy or beauty. Dead cows ain't pretty, and they aren't any better when they are gold-plated or getting sprinkled with salt by a man with a ponytail. What gold-plated steaks are is rich... and you're poor (sorry, that's just a reflex at this point). They are a rich thing covered in a rich thing, served to rich people by a rich man who gives you a receipt to photograph at the end. The joy is completely performative and what beauty there happens to be is a very cold version of what beauty can be. In my opinion, it's beauty in the advertising and marketing sense. 'Beauty' that is trying *so hard*, it becomes ugly. It's like Donald Trump bought Angus Steakhouses in 1986 and then got the guy from *American Psycho* to oversee the customer experience. Food without cooking, community or taste. Which means, it is not really food at all any more, it is theatre. Really bad, really expensive theatre.

Some people prefer to showcase 'joy' through food on the Internet, which has its own kind of really bad, really expensive theatre too. The foods being eaten are usually

---

[8] In my case, it is with increasing XP in bitterness, shade and Ibegyourpardons.

sweet, as in sugary, and sweet, as in *Awww*. The thing being eaten should ideally be squidgy and have a cute and well-designed face that showcases expensive and time-consuming attention to detail. This allows someone with good teeth to bite into the cute face and feel joy. It is your classic 'Biting a Face and Feeling Joy'-type scenario. Nothing odd about that. If you're wondering about presentation, just go for the polar opposite of Salt Bae, so instead of a dominatrix, guillotine-sharpening theme, choose something with lots of icing and bright colours. Go for a child's idea of feminine imagery rather than a grown man's meathead art project.

The key to *joyful* expressions is simplicity. You want to seem like a simpleton, but also to show you have childlike, simple joy in your life. The presentation is usually quite *Animal Crossing*, with a funny, upbeat theme song and very few words. It is adult life as designed by a child who wants to be a princess. Some who have delusions of maturity choose to showcase their joy with the elaborate preparation of tea or iced coffee. By introducing caffeine into the mix, the child (here played by an adult influencer) can really play grown-ups by pretending to require a stimulant. It is the same impulse that drives small children to have tea parties with their dolls, but in place of dolls there are three million people watching on a phone and the process of making tea or iced coffee is unreasonably expensive and complicated.

Let me run you through the process of *joyfully* making some tea to show to the world online (and your dolls if you like). You will need a sort of chemistry kit involving stacking what look like three or four Pyrex jugs on top of one another. The one at the top should have some sort of small green ball of tea leaves in it. When this has boiling water poured over it, it should magically transform into some sort of alien flower that turns the water green. I am serious about the alien flower bit – if your tea ball doesn't expand and appear to have claws and branches then no one will care. Once the water is green, you should twist a knob or push a lever so that the water flows down into another Pyrex jug. This is most likely an ornamental Pyrex. Its purpose is just to create more drama on the way down to your clear teapot. Think of this layering as something Wallace from Wallace and Gromit would add just to show off the kinds of skills you can develop if your primary social interactions are with a mute but very capable dog. Your tea flows from this Wallace waiting room to your pot, which is also unnecessary, because you're just gonna pour it into a cup.

Or is it? Because your cup may or may not have bally ice cubes (yes, we're going to get to them) and by putting it in a pot for three seconds first, you have somehow prepared it for the icing stage. OK, now you can put it in the cup. It meets your round ice and forms a lukewarm, slightly watery version of the alien claw tea that you just prepared. And it's BEAUTIFUL. You feel a lot of joy, and the people who look to you for Pyrex, alien tea joy feel it as well, but now they are done with you. They are bored and they feel they need more. You MUST keep them here. So you give them more.

You throw away your Wallace and Gromit tea and decide to make a coffee. Nescafé? NespressNO, more like. This coffee will need to be different. Ideally, you will have access to that coffee which has been eaten and pooed out by a something-or-other cat. You think I'm joking don't you. Bless your ~~cotton nylon~~ hessian socks, you don't even know about something-or-other cat poo coffee. It's about £40 for a small bag (125g), if you're getting the cheap kind, and it's really good for showing that you are joyful, caffeinated and rich. The process behind this coffee is quite simple: coffee berries (yeah I know, berries!)

fall on the ground and get eaten by civet cats. They then poo out partially digested coffee beans, which get made into really expensive coffee. I honestly would go on a rant but I think that really says it all. The most expensive coffee in the world is collected from civet cat poo and you can't afford it. So you want to use those beans, ideally, but if you're poor or don't breed civets and have a coffee plantation, then you will have to use *undigested* coffee.

So get your undigested coffee and make some coffee. That sounds simple and it is, so you'll have to make it look complicated by using gravity or shaved glacier ice or something else that Wallace has going spare and then add some other random stuff. This final part is key: you'll wanna get some matcha or something else colourful and mix it all in until the drink looks disgusting. It is really important that the drink looks weird and memorable, because that's the only way you're gonna compete with someone who brewed theirs with the help of a civet's bum. Now you add it to some ice and get a big straw, because that is how you show you are different from normal people. They drink brown coffee with their mouth, but you drink green coffee with a straw, so you are worth staring at. You are a source of joy.

And you are the decline of Western civilisation. And Eastern civilisation, to be fair, as it seems like Asia has a thing for performative hot drinks being iced as well. If you can just follow these easy steps to make having a drink really hard, you can be on the Internet. You can look rich and be rich and have a joyful and beautiful online avatar. Congratulations. Or you can just have a cup of bumhole-free tea or coffee and be a povvo. It's a blue pill/red pill situation and I think we both know you have chosen truth. I, Shaborpheus, have held out a civet coffee bean and a bog-standard brown teabag and you have chosen the tea. Let it be spilt. It is time to talk povvo, because I've had enough of these rich people. I want to discuss what the rest of us do with our food and drink.

...

But, Shabaaaaaz [It's Shaborpheus now!], *you said you were gonna talk about ice cubes.* I know, but I'm saving them for Chapter 8 because I think ice cubes are more about order and cleanliness than food or even drink. I have a whole taxonomy for this laughing at rich people thing, so you'll just have to trust me. Trust me like you trust the milk you sniff in the fridge. I may look out of date, and I may just be sour, but give me a sniff and see how it goes. You won't regret it.

OK, as anyone who sniffs the milk knows well, you might regret it, but use all that trust you have saved up from not trusting best before dates to stick with me. That is just a recommendation, much like the best before date itself. My mother taught me never to trust them, that they are a conspiracy cooked up by Big Farmer/Big Supermarket to make us waste good food and buy more. She says they don't exist in Pakistan and who am I to argue with my mother? Her attitude is that food is either being eaten now or frozen for later, and that leaves no room for things being off or passing their best before date. It is best now, and best frozen and defrosted later.

I never really understood why she needed three freezers in the house (bougie, I know) until we moved and we had to clear them out. What I found was a culinary time machine/nightmare. I found a cake from my fourth birthday, curry that had outlasted five prime ministers and a frozen chicken that had once been on a farm with Dolly the sheep.[9] I can only assume she thinks

---

[9] The original one.

like one of those crazy rich guys that gets themselves cryogenically frozen in the hope that future technology will be advanced enough for them to bring themselves back to life someday, but with halal meat products, not, as legend has it, Walt Disney's body. If there is a mad scientist out there who can bring cryogenically frozen lamb chops back to life after 30 years, then come to mine. Dinner's on us.

I think disaster preparation and cryogenic freezing are a couple of areas where the super-rich and povvos actually meet in the middle. While Mark Zuckerberg and his tech billionaire bros are (allegedly) preparing for the apocalypse by buying up bunkers in New Zealand, my mum is cold-storing a century's worth of choc ices in Blackburn in preparation for the Rapture. Someday, the two communities will come together. I imagine it will be in the form of a reality show that is a bit like *Wife Swap* for the 22nd century.

NARRATOR: Mark is 104 years old, a software engineer by trade, he has been living in a state-of-the-art bunker for the past 63 years, surviving on fungus that his servants cultivate. But now, in this groundbreaking series, he's going to discover how the other half live.

Mark has traversed the earth through a series of underground tunnels to spend two weeks living with the Ali family in Blackburn.

Welcome to *Apocalypse Swap*.

Cuts to scene of Mark trying a samosa from 1998 and looking impressed.

MARK: I'm actually going to stay here. I appreciate that my servants in New Zealand will miss me, but the Ali family and their 16 freezers have made me feel so welcome, and I just can't go back to eating cultivated fungus.

Cue scene of servants in New Zealand celebrating.

I can't say how this apocalypse will come, but if it's in the form of a global food shortage, we'll be fine; if it's disease, maybe less so. If it's global warming, then we may be to blame, because of this povvo hack: **leave the oven door open after cooking to warm up the house.**

This hack has a powerful message. It is motivated by all the same concerns as the other cheapskate shortcuts we will be discussing, but it's almost scientific in its clarity. It's physics for povvos: you've bought heat; that same heat can cook food and, later, warm your home. Simple. Yes, your home might smell like lasagne for a few days and, yes, sometimes there is a smoky tinge to your hallway afterwards, but nothing smells better than a nice low heating bill. So, suck it up. That heat is yours. Use it, you earnt it.

If I had to lay a bet on which people utilise the extraordinary power of the oven to be a secondary boiler, I would say that they are mostly the same people who have a healthy respect for and fear of their fridge-freezer. These, I know only too well from my own experience, are the domestic scientists who will start to scream if the fridge door is left open too long or, God forbid, THE FREEZER. The power of the freezer must not be underestimated, the freezer freezeth and the freezer taketh away heat… from the rest of the house, apparently. I can only assume that my mother has undertaken painstaking research on the freezer heat vortex to determine her 8-second limit for opening times.

It might just be that she respects the freezer because she understands its power – after all, she is the woman who has a Fab ice lolly from 1988 (still in its *original* packaging, for any would-be buyers out there). Of course, some tension arises from the fact that my mum has 28 years' worth of food in the freezer, but won't allow you to look through it for more than 8 seconds. It is nearly impossible to find anything in a library that size in that amount of time. Comparable treasure troves, such as the British Library or the vaults of the Natural History Museum, have systems in place to help you traverse their storied corridors, but it can still take hours to find the artefacts you are looking for. My mum's freezer does not have a system. It has ice all around the things you are looking for and an inbuilt system that slaps the lid closed after the 8-second limit passes, called M.U.M.

I appreciate that, much like the curators of museums, she has priceless artefacts to protect and, just as Leonardo da Vinci manuscripts can be damaged by light, Millennium Kebabs can be ruined by heat. She respects her art and her money and, like all great povvos, there is an art to her cheapness. Take the following mantra, for example: **use any tub with a lid to store food.**

There is nothing artier, more beautiful and frustrating than empty margarine tubs repurposed for leftovers. They are more colourful than the boring Tupperware that the middle classes have been tricked into buying. Margarine tubs are free. And they are infuriating. They stack up in the fridge and freezer, bringing a riot of colour to your white goods and offering an element of jeopardy to any trip to either. Say it's a hot day. You've done a few 7.9-second opens of the freezer to see what is inside. The M.U.M. alarm has not been tripped. You notice a tub of Neapolitan ice cream – the famous combination of chocolate, strawberry and white (vanilla? not really) that the people of Naples proudly named themselves after. You are ecstatic. To maintain the freeze, you run upstairs (the freezer is kept in the basement to protect foods from UV damage) and prepare your bowl, spoon, strawberry sauce and sprinkles. *This is living*, you think. *I am so alive.* You run back downstairs, pull out the ice cream and carry it to the kitchen. With cold fingers and a warm heart, you pop open your prize… to find it's filled with last week's chicken korma. You just have some sauce and sprinkles instead.

This is the art of the repurposed tub. Much like life, it is opaque and obscure. It doesn't offer the clarity of Tupperware, but it leaves your existence the more colourful for it. It is also, obviously, more stressful. The pinnacle of this stress comes in the sort of body-swap comedy offered by margarine and other tubs.

As the most common of the tubs repurposed for storage, margarine tubs have the potential to trap you in a sort of 'I AM SPARTACUS!' slapstick comedy in which you are unsure of the one true margarine. This is most pronounced around toast, when the need to get to margarine in a timely manner is particularly pressing. You have timed your toast perfectly – it's a 6.3 on the 'bread to toast' scale (just how you like it) – and you know that getting margarine on it as quickly as possible is the key to a good end product. You swing open the fridge door. There are 16 margarine tubs. You play an increasingly frustrating game of Whac-A-Mole in which you are popping caps on tubs to find curries, pasta, mint sauce, yogurt, desserts and every foodstuff that is not

This is the art of the repurposed tub. Much like life, it is opaque and obscure. It doesn't offer the clarity of Tupperware, but it leaves your existence the more colourful for it.

margarine. Opening the 16th margarine tub, you realise that there actually isn't any. There is the appearance of an absolute abundance of it, but a reality in which there is none. You consider throwing away one of the tubs as an act of defiance, then you remember, Mum hasn't spoken to an aunty for 10 years because she lost her Tupperware. You like Mum. So you have yogurt and mint sauce on toast. It is all right. The addition of left-over sprinkles helps.

These stories make my life sound quite sad. It isn't. It just has some *perspective*. We can't all have ice cream and toast when we want it and that's that. Nothing to be sad about there. If you do happen to be rich and reading all this feeling sorry for me,[10] I recommend you skip the next povvo hack as it might just send you over the edge: **sleep for dinner.**

This one is for the povvOGs. It sounds a bit like abuse, and it may feel like it at the time, but usually it is not. Generally, in my experience, it is a tactic I turn to when I am too lazy to cook or feel like I could save on expenses by going into hibernation mode. As a child, it was usually a response to the line, 'I don't want X for dinner' or 'I'm still hungry' and rarely followed through. Disclaimer: sleep for dinner is recommended by 0/10 dieticians and 0 per cent of parenting experts. This is not proper dietary advice, although it sounds like something a Tory Cabinet minister might recommend for those struggling with the cost of living crisis.

Next hack: **rinse the jar or tin to get every bit of what's inside it.**

This, however, is crucial domestic advice. To those of you who have lived bougie from day one, it might seem shocking, and I was certainly shocked the first time I saw my mother

---

10 Gofundme.com/getshabazsomelurpak

rinsing the bottom of a can of beans, then adding it to the pot. I told her I didn't want any bean water. She told me she'd been doing it my whole life, and I accepted that the bean water may actually be the tastiest part. This advice is actually useful across the condiment spectrum. Rinse your ketchup, your brown sauce, maybe even your Roy's Sister Sheree.[11] The bits at the bottom of any saucepot are the most flavourful and, when diluted with tap water, you can actually get subtle notes and undertones that you may have otherwise missed.

A close relation of sauce rinsing is bottom tapping (which sounds like Gen Z slang for intercourse). This approach can be most easily summed up by the povvoqualism: **turn it upside down to get everything out.**

It is a little-known fact that this was actually the inspiration for Diana Ross and Nile Rogers' classic 'Upside down', which was written from the perspective of a Reggae Reggae sauce bottle. OK, it wasn't, but it should have been. Too few artists try to capture the perspective of condiments. 'Turn it upside down' usually predates 'Rinse it out' by about a week, which is testament to just how much can be achieved with these tactics. After the turn, you usually have the shake, the bottom tap, the bottom slap, the more vigorous shake and the dreaded 'swizzle a knife around in there', which we all know is a recipe for disappointment. If you have a knife in your hand, put it down. It's time to rinse.

For any povvo fortunate enough to eat outside their home (in my childhood this generally meant packing a duffel bag with 63 samosas to eat at a playground, but here I mean *a restaurant*), another rinse comes naturally. Rinse the

---

11 If you do not understand, then google these words with my name. All will become clear. If you are called Sheree and have a brother called Roy, don't worry, you haven't secretly become a meme.

establishment you visit by taking any sachets they offer you as part of their business. A povvo on my page reported gleefully about the time she almost refilled an entire bottle of soy sauce with those mini plastic soy sauce fishes that they give out at Japanese restaurants. That is like a loyalty card for legends/absolute states. I would like to ask her whether she was regularly going for sushi or just came in like a trawler fisherman one day and hoovered up the whole soy sauce sea of its plastic fish? I hope it was the latter.

Another and arguably most fun of the povvo hacks that have been suggested on my page is **the 10-second rule**, which combines cheapness and questionable hygiene practices in a fun game format.

This is particularly useful if you are too poor to have games. I have heard it called the 5-second rule (I imagine it was Marie Antoinette or someone who came up with that) and I have tried to lobby for a 15-second one, but people seem set on the 10-second version. I considered not including this, as I thought everyone did it, until I saw my rich friend throw away a bagel because she had dropped it on the floor. I then realised that not everyone understands the 'science' behind this rule. As I am a science teacher, I will explain (though, spoiler alert: I will be using none of my hard-earned knowledge to do so).

All germs and bacteria have a built-in '10-second rule', which means that they don't latch on to ground-based foodstuff for a minimum of 10 seconds. This is a quirk of evolution that we in the scientific community are still trying to understand. Under a microscope, it is fascinating to watch. A delicious cheesy biscuit can be placed in a Petri dish and you can actually see the E. coli biting its lip and tapping its feet on the ground as it waits for the 10 seconds to be up. As researchers, we generally let them keep the treat because they have waited so patiently.

Of course, that's not true. It is true, however, that my rich friend has genuinely never eaten anything she dropped on the floor, and I can only assume that she is deeply unhealthy and has a dangerously weak immune system as a result. This is also not scientifically verified but I believe it.

Finally, we have: **compare the price per kg.**

Obviously. It has been said of many a misanthrope that they know the price of everything and the value of nothing. Well, sorry, Quotes.com, but you need to know the price of everything to know the value of anything, so maybe you are only trying to justify shopping at Waitrose or M&S.

The level above knowing the price of everything (and therefore actually *becoming* value in human form) is knowing the price *per kg* of everything. At this point, you are a sort of supermarket savant, able to filter out anything being sold in units smaller than about 5kg. You find yourself becoming stronger (it's the lifting), mentally dextrous (it's the calculations) and popular at checkouts (as you can only physically transport about three items per shopping trip). When you elevate yourself to this mindstate, we say you have reached 'povvo+' and your heightened consciousness will see you inducted into the Costco Hall of Fame, respected by even the most critical aunties.

You will finally know your true value. Your price per kg.

Because you are what you eat.

BEG YOUR PAR
ROUND BALLY IC
RICH, YOU'RE PO
POKEN LIKE A
POVVO, BECAUS
OT AN ANIMAL
VHY?, BECAUSE
OU'RE A POVVO
VHAT ON GOD'S
ARTH, ON TODA
PISODE OF..., RO
ISTER SHERRIE
AVE A DAY OFF
ASP...STOP IT I

BEAUTY
FIFTY SHADES OF BEIGE

Right at the heart of 1D's song 'What Makes You Beautiful' lies one of life's greatest paradoxes – a concept in theoretical physics first postulated by Erwin Schrödinger and, later, by Niall Horan. It is the incredibly depressing reality that everyone is either ugly or feels ugly. You see, in a paper (2011),[1] the team discusses how the subject of the study is beautiful because they do not know that they are. Should the subject become aware of their beauty and stop feeling ugly, they immediately cease to be beautiful. This means that we must always either feel ugly or be ugly, and I am proud to say that my theories in this chapter largely build on the research of these great scientists. I am standing on the shoulders of giants.

This is one way of saying that beauty, when presented on the Internet, immediately becomes ugly because it's one thing to know you're beautiful, but another to monetise it. This also means that the rest of us who do not present our beauty on the Internet (because we feel ugly) must be absolute blooming stunners, which is fantastic news, and I should probably leave it there because, if I keep going, you're gonna start

◀◀ ▶▶

The real paradox is that the way beauty can be presented on the Internet is ugly. It can be an ugly business, full of beautiful people selling us different ways to become more like them, when, confusingly (again), beauty is something that you can't really buy.

---

[1] Styles, Malik, Schrödinger et al. (2011) *Not Nature*.

believing in yourself and Louis Tomlinson will turn up at your house and tell you you're a four. Sadly, you will have to accept your onrushing downgrade because I have a chapter to write, and it's OK because, once you feel ugly again, you'll become beautiful and the cycle can begin once more.

This is not a real paradox, so there's no need to worry. The real paradox is that the way beauty can be presented on the Internet is ugly. It can be an ugly business, full of beautiful people selling us different ways to become more like them, when, confusingly (again), beauty is something that you can't really buy. You are literally born with it,[2] and if you are lucky enough to be born with it, you can try to convince other people to buy it from you, safe in the knowledge that, although they can pay, they can't have it. They will be repeat customers and you will keep selling. It is the perfect business model that can see you through from your teenage years, selling redundant concealer, to your later ones, selling redundant anti-wrinkle cream. You could even remain a force after your death, marketing embalming fluids and grave wax to ugly normies who have hardly any followers on their funeral live stream. This has the added benefit that, when the zombie apocalypse arrives, everyone will be chased around by perfectly smooth, undead beings chanting 'Just Woke Up Like This'.

The phrase 'Just Woke Up Like This' actually gets to the core of the problem with beauty on the Internet. It is the first lie from which all the others extend because the simple fact is that anyone 'with it' enough to take a photo is already more awake and ready than someone who actually just woke up. Waking up is an experience of extreme confusion,

---

[2] It's not Maybelline.

disorientation and dread. Our brains are effectively newborn and our faces are a mixture of shock and fear. The only real example of 'Just Woke Up Like This' would be achieved by sneaking into the homes of influencers and prodding them awake with a selfie stick, then capturing the moment of existential dread as their eyes opened to a flash and my grinning face. This would be a powerful image and a wonderful way to spend my last morning as a free man before the police arrived. It would also bring some reality back to proceedings because, if you have managed to take a photo and you have a camera to hand, then you have not just woken up like this.

The camera itself is also often helpful. Modern cameras make us look good, even if we want to believe that 'I always look so bad in photos'. This can be confusing. Looking at a 2D representation of our 3D self is odd, and we think that we don't look like ourselves, because we don't. I am not Flat Stanley,[3] I have dimensions, but the truth is, I would be better off saying, 'I look bad in 2D'[4] than 'I look bad in photos'. What people mean when they say, 'I look bad in photos' is, 'I don't look like how I'm trying to look in photos'. That is because they are not doing the face they do for photos, the one that makes them look more like the 'photo-me' they want to look like, which, in turn, is more like people on the Internet.

This is because people have got very used to doing a certain face for pictures that is nothing like their normal face, so when they are photographed not doing that face, they feel

---

[3] Look him up. He posted himself in an envelope. Power move.
[4] Not to be confused with looking bad to 1D, the scientists discussed at the start of the chapter. I don't know what it means if they think you look bad. It might mean you are really beautiful. More research is needed.

like they look bad or less like themselves. In reality, the photo-face self looks least like we actually do all the rest of the time. The only way this system could work is if we walked around pouting *all* the time, making peace signs and looking slightly above other people's eyes. We would have bad backs from sticking out our bums and sucking in our tummies, and the fundamental physiology of our mouths would change as then we would only smile with our eyes, but at least we would look like we do in photos.

I don't know what we would do for photos at that point, because we would want to look better in those than we do in real life. That may be where filters would come in again to save the day. But before we get on to them, I want to dwell a bit more on how we picture ourselves. It feels sort of important. So, to start, do you remember the time before we all had photos of ourselves all the time? Many millennia ago, back in about 2008. For those of you too young to remember, I feel both pity and envy. Pity that you have grown up in a world where seeing yourself photographed 10 times a day is normal; envy that you probably still look really young and sweet. Well, sweet child, before about 2010, people didn't take photos very often and, as a result, we didn't really know what to do in them. When you were in a photo, you either made a funny face (because, 'What is this weird situation I am in? Being photographed?') or did a really wholesome genuine graduation photo smile. You either had an expression like a bad children's entertainer or someone collecting their degree certificate. There was no effort made to look effortlessly hot. You wouldn't be able to look at the picture and judge it immediately, and you wouldn't be able to take another one, so you either wanted something that looked funny   enough   to   laugh   at   with   your   friends   or intergenerationally satisfying enough to go on your grandma's wall. There was no time for being sexy. Which is for the best as I was about 14.

If you are about 14 now, that whole section will seem very odd. You have grown up in a world where you see people trying to look sexy all the time, so you probably think there is nothing strange about children trying to be sexy. You will probably also feel that filters – those things which make us look sexy, like children or sexy cartoon children – are normal too. They absolutely are not. I'm not saying they are *wrong* or it should be illegal to look like a saucy strawberry, but filters are not normal. In fact, I think filters are abnormal, and are doing a heap of damage to our self-image. They are essentially a race to the bottom. We apply one filter to make us look nicer, and the reality of ourselves without the filter immediately looks worse. We then feel even more dependent on the filters, and we want more of them to help us bridge the gap with our reality. Down and down we go until the only version of ourselves that we feel comfortable with has a pretty cat face and the one we are stuck with the rest of the time is a burden. This is destructive to our sense of self, but it is even worse when you consider that we spend a large portion of our remaining time looking at people who are ALREADY beautiful posting pictures of themselves with filters that make them look *even* better. So then we feel bad about our real self looking worse than our filtered one, and our filtered one looking so much worse than a beautiful person's.

If only we could go back to the good old days of there being some professionally attractive people who had pictures taken of them (called models) and everyone else who existed in the real world. Now we are playing the same game as the models but we are destined to lose. Unless we buy some products, that is. Then maybe, just maybe, we will win. Which, of course, we won't. The sad truth is that no beauty products can make you beautiful. If they could, they would stop making new ones, and the people who owned the companies would all just employ themselves to advertise them, rather than people who looked nice already.

The message they give out is that if you buy their products, you will look young and beautiful, right? So if you had the money and bought the products, you would look amazing, right? Well, apparently, the richest woman in the world when she died in 2017 had inherited the L'Oréal fortune from her father and was one of the principal shareholders of the company. She had all the money and access to, literally, loads of beauty products. She also had a perfectly normal number of wrinkles for a woman of 94. To me, we can take this as evidence that neither cash nor toiletries can make you look young. If close to $40 billion and every L'Oréal product she could ever ask for couldn't do it for her, faffing £12 on cream ain't gonna either. We should all give up now. No toiletries, no filters.

We would have to coordinate because only by giving up at the same time would we all remain in the same place relatively. If everyone stopped wearing make-up or using filters together, then everyone would look about 0.2 per cent worse and no one would notice because everyone would change an equal amount. We would all be like men. Well, like men were from about 1840 until 2015. Men who didn't know how good they had it. (When I say 'men', I mean blokes, which is why I am using 'they'. I'm not exactly a card-carrying member of the blokes.) Men have had nearly two hundred years without any of the pressure to 'be beautiful' that women experience every day. Before that, back in the

Georgian era (the bad old days, just before Myspace), blokes were getting glammed up beyond belief, and the jealousy one bro could feel when another bro had exactly the shade of lead face-whitening powder he coveted was REAL. They likely all got mercury poisoning from making their own rouge and it became a nuclear arms race to see who could get the highest white Marge Simpson hair hat. Then they stopped. All of a sudden, they all stopped (or at least, it seems that way to me, OK historians?!). I don't know if they had a conference or a war to speed up the decision (these are the two male options), but when they became Victorians, they concentrated instead on starchy suits and big beards. They looked a bit worse, but they all did it *together* so lost nothing while saving massively on lead poisoning and fop-envy.

They must have had another conference alongside the wars at the start of the twentieth century because the 1900s ushered in the golden age of male beauty. For the next 100 years, film stars were fundamentally average-looking blokes like John Wayne, superheroes had paunches and the two clothing styles were 'work' or 'pub'. Male grooming was shaving – not trimming or shaping, *just* shaving. Then along came *GQ*, David Beckham and co., plus a load of execs from companies that had already tried selling all the cosmetic products to women, and it was decided to have a go at selling to the other lot. The result was the male grooming routines of social media.

These are essentially the same as the female ones, but they just add some weights in the background and don't show the bit where they put on make-up. A key difference is that the ingredients in their products have to be horrible, like charcoal, brandy or leather (which, ironically, is probably what the older blokes smelt like for free), and the packaging has to be black. Whereas women's cosmetics are marketed as though their customers are kids in a sweet shop, men's brands imagine that their customers want to be in a factory, smoking, drinking brandy and tanning leather. The men in the grooming videos do not look like they smoke, drink or work in a tannery, though. They are basically more muscular versions of the women who do beauty tutorials, so that when the AI replaces us all, it can just use the same faces and swap out the boobs.

The men's grooming videos have an advanced level, which involves beard care. This requires oils, which should also smell like smoke, leather or wood (apparently), and star men who would probably look a bit nicer without giant beards showing how they tame their giant beards. The beards are a bit like Tamagotchis, in that these men pay to have something they need to take care of and talk about, but which provides little tangible benefit to them. It is incredible to me that a whole industry has managed to grow off the back of beard videos, and even more incredible that it spawned another industry – 'manscaping' – for what grows on the back of it and below. While it is amusing to see male body hair finally being policed in the way that women's has for a few hundred years, the marketing-speak which has developed around intimate male hair removal is terrible enough to undo any of the goodwill that the new-found equality has generated in me. Unfortunately, it seems that men can only be sold products that trim their body hair ironically and with references to hard labour. As a result, the devices used have names like 'crop trimmer' and 'the shed'. There is also, apparently, ball deodorant. The less said about that the better, but if the algorithm could stop suggesting it as a 'great gift for dads, sons or brothers', I would be eternally grateful and so made up, I would invest in viral body hair-trimming products for the next 30 years. That's a promise. I would even call male make-up 'warpaint', like the Internet wants me to.

Make-up tutorials, or extremely long cosmetics adverts as they used to be known, require far more intellect than beard tutorials. Men are still operating at the toddler stage of grooming whereas beauty influencers are out there with doctorates in the subject. While most men are learning to put things on their face (like babies), there are artists using foundation to make themselves look like entirely different people. Obviously, such people are extremely attractive to those of us who have had our self-image distorted by the Internet. I think that the Internet cosmetics industry treats young women in a similar way to how crypto/investor socials approach teenage boys. You find people who feel inadequate because everyone seems beautiful or rich, then you show them someone with skills and materials that they don't have, which makes them appear more beautiful and richer. Once you have done this, you tell them to buy knock-off versions[5] of the materials you used, and leave them feeling even worse and poorer when they fail to do as well as you did in the video.

This is assuming that you even have skills. If you lack them, there is an even simpler option, but you will need to already have money. This is simply buying all of the make-up and showing it to people. You will need at least fifty shades of beige, from every different brand, and you will have to organise these in a way that really shows your mastery of the

---

[5] Since rebranded as 'dupes', in the same way that 'second-hand' is now 'preloved'. If that is true, then I have worn a *whole* lotta love in my lifetime.

entire costly beige spectrum. If you have cash, a camera and some hands, you can genuinely make money out of the jealousy you create. I highly recommend this approach if you also happen to have hoarding tendencies, as I am convinced all of us do.[6] It gives you an effective way to monetise your hoarding by taking the raw materials of your compulsion and converting them into someone else's. Your compulsive hoarding can become someone else's compulsive buying, and then you are officially a functioning member of a capitalist society, with followers.

I don't imagine that this is a path *you* are going to take, judging from the absolute outrage in response to my videos when I have showcased monetised hoarding. In fact, most of the responses to these videos centre on the actual shelf-life of make-up, whether mascara can qualify as an heirloom and our impending ecological crisis. This is why I love you, and why it's time we stopped discussing all the people who are trying to sell a dream on the Internet and started talking about all the ways in which you aren't buying it. I've done the maths and, by my calculations, one online make-up hoarding influencer could keep 1 million povvogang members in make-up for life, because you hoard knowledge, not mascara, and with that knowledge you flourish.

I would argue that knowledge, know-how and savvy are the hallmarks of a povvo. I've been thinking a lot about what it means to be a povvo (you can tell I'm a busy guy) and it all comes down to having some sense. If you have a bit of self-awareness, if you can tell when you're being sold to and you actually care about the way other people feel as a result of

---

6 I'd argue that Marie Kondo is not an organiser, she is a therapist.

your actions, you're a povvo. It's not just about having or not having money; it's about having sense. That's why these chapters aren't just about wealth; they are about smarts, self-image and community. I want to see a more equal society, but I also want to see one where people are a little bit sharper about the information they take in and the attention they give. This is my povvo manifesto.

If you have a bit of self-awareness, if you can tell when you're being sold to and you actually care about the way other people feel as a result of your actions, you're a povvo.

I know Karl Marx sort of tried to do the whole povvo manifesto thing, albeit with a few minor differences,[7] but he didn't have any parts about getting the sticky bits out of the bottom of a tube of mascara, so I think our one is more relevant to life and has greater potential to have a positive impact on the world than his one ever did. So I bring you a povvo tip: **using hot water to get the last of any beauty product out of its container.**

Entry-level povvo beauty that. I'm surprised Karl never tried it. He was a few thick lashes away from really getting the globe to embrace his ideas. Hot water is a straightforward solution to an incredibly annoying situation, a situation that probably leads people to anger-buy more mascara than they would ever need. The highest form of this approach is, of course, to warm some water[8] in the oven that you have used previously for cooking, as this creates a povvo beauty–food

---

[7] OK, OK, *many* differences, but you get my point.

continuum. This trick works for glass or hard containers, but if you are wanting to get at a product which is in packaging that is soft enough: **cut the top off to get to those last few squeezes you know are in there.**

Otherwise known as squeeze every last drop you can out of life... and moisturiser. This small habit could have life-changing consequences. It is a way of saying, 'I want to get what I deserve, I need to live life to the fullest, I need to maximise (my Max Factor).' You may find yourself demanding a well-deserved pay rise after you do this, finding a relationship built on true equality and sorting out global tax evasion by major corporations. You may just get a bit more concealer. All of those are good things. This tip is closely related to: **adding some nail varnish remover to the bottom of a varnish bottle to get the extra bits from the bottom.**

This provides the added satisfaction of using something that usually taketh away to giveth. It feels like creating something out of less than something, and you can enjoy the heady rush that alchemists have sought for millenia.

The povvo (judging from your suggestions for this book) is both an alchemist and an engineer, a budget version of the bio-hacking billionaire who, instead of trying to make themselves live for ever/look 12 at 47, tries to turn soap into a renewable resource. This is what I meant about knowledge. Our society may not value **creating new bars of soap by smooshing together slivers** in the way it values cold fusion or the pursuit of eternal life but, intellectually, I think they are on a par. We probably need to just give this tip a better name,

---

8 You may even want to just mix that water in with the product, too, if you are desperate enough. After all, 71 per cent of the planet is water, so your foundation can be too.

some better *branding*, like calling it 'Warm Fusion' or the 'Pursuit of Eternal Life (soap)' and we'll get the research funding and academic kudos we deserve. I don't know if it is entrenched elitism, the patriarchy or their fear of our might that stops our wisdom from becoming mainstream science. It might be because our theories have sometimes shared platforms with unsavoury views. That is why I will only give a small mention to the suggestion **steal loo rolls**. This is truly revolutionary and, as we seek more mainstream approval, we may need to distance ourselves as povvos from our more militant wing of toilet roll stealers. I am not saying this kind of (loo roll) armed uprising never has a place, but we might have to keep our affiliations unofficial. If you need to steal toilet paper, though, I can see a time when it may be justifiable.

Samples was a tip that came in a few times. One word, endless possibilities. I like to imagine all of you who suggested it passing through well-stocked beauty counters like Baloo from *The Jungle Book*, singing the song 'The Bare Necessities' but, instead of looking under rocks and plants in search of the fanciest ants (and the fancier the better), you pick up one of every sample from every counter. I don't know whether our militant faction of toilet roll takers would be willing to just take *samples* of toilet rolls rather than whole rolls, and whether this would fundamentally change the activity. It is one for the committee to discuss. The elite levels of sample manipulation involve either pocketing a whole dresser-worth of sample tubs (two each, go in a group) or moving from counter to counter until you have a full face of make-up. This will take some planning and navigation, but I believe in you.

Navigating the world of retail is a science and an art for a povvo. We want to be smarter than the marketers. We want to understand the machinery they have created to manipulate our desires, to come out of a Boots or a Superdrug (or a drugstore – hi, American readers!) with what we need rather than what they want us to want. The first level of this is how we shop. I've had povvos tell me, *'Never shop at eye level'*, which sounds like a bit of a povspiracy theory at first, but is based in fact. The brands pay more to be located at eye level, and they pass the cost of that on to you and me. Hidden down at the bottom of the shelf is an array of bigger, better and cheaper products that don't have 'the eye-level tax' priced into them. Real eyes, realise, real lies about reels of eycliners.

So first we refuse the structure behind the shopping experience, then we elevate and refuse the structure of product distinctions. I can't tell you how much povspiration (sounds like sweat, not gonna keep using that one) I have received about **treating beauty products interchangeably.** Lipstick can be blusher, blusher can be eyeshadow. Eyeshadow can be brow filler, brow filler can be eyeliner. Eyeshadow can be highlighter and lipstick and foundation combined can make a cream blusher. This is high-functioning beauty. This is the beauty of high function. This is what happens when lots of smart people who don't want to buy things, defy lots of smart people who want them to. What we create is

I've had povvos tell me, 'Never shop at eye level', which sounds like a bit of a povspiracy theory at first, but is based in fact. The brands pay more to be located at eye level, and they pass the cost of that on to you and me.

something more. It is evolution in action. What we really need to do, as a team, is to try to isolate a sort of Swiss army knife of beauty – two or three products that, together, can combine to create every possible aesthetic outcome. This is a bit above my level, as I am not the scientist that you all seem to be, but when you discover this tool kit, I'm putting it out into the world.

There is also a very thin line between mad science projects and 'natural beauty' regimes. I've seen apple cider vinegar and baking soda shampoo concoctions, as well as all manner of things using castor oil, but my favourite food/science/beauty combo is: **making beauty masks with whatever is in the fridge/on the counter.**

You know that one of those repurposed margarine tubs has something unctuous in it, you know some of those foodstuffs could have been mentioned by Gwyneth Paltrow on Goop,[9] so go ahead and make a coconut raita facial mask (that actually sounds good). Avoid spices and anything too brightly coloured/heavily scented and you're good. Garlic butter face mask may not work, but yogurt and mint go together just fine. If the food is a bit off, then even better – it's a 'live' face mask, with probiotic cultures rigorously proven to boost skin bombasticity.[10] Yes, you smell a bit, but there is a glow that goes with your hum. People will believe in you and you can say 'my skin adviser'[11] put this together for me based on my requirements (those being: (1) what was there; (2) what wasn't too smelly; (3) what was there and not too smelly).

Finally, obviously, and probably completely unnecessarily, given that you are making your own face masks and robbing

----

[9] As if they are NEW. My ancestors knew about turmeric. Thank you very much. Grandma is turning in her grave and SHE'S NOT EVEN DEAD.
[10] If you do your own marketing as well, then you are set.
[11] Whoever is nearest the fridge.

loo rolls: **don't buy promotions.**

Two for the price of one, DO ONE/BOGOF... literally...
bog off. If you can give me two of them, then you could do
it half price. I only need one perfume, thank you (unless
your skin adviser opted for the shrimp paste in your mask).
Promotions are a lie, and we have all known that ever since
we were about ten and realised that some furniture sales
were ALWAYS ON. You can't have a half-price sale *all* the
time, we know you just have a whole land of oak furniture
that you need to shift and you're acting like you are doing us
a favour. And, supermarkets, you can't just charge more and
call the old price a 'clubcard' one. This will not fly. We know
better.

Because knowledge is power. And knowledge is beauty.
So you are all beautiful enough as you are.

Oh no, I shouldn't have said that. I've just seen Zayn
Malik and he wants to tell us we're all munters again.

BEG YOUR PAR
ROUND BALLY IC
RICH, YOU'RE PO
SPOKEN LIKE A
POVVO, BECAUS
NOT AN ANIMAL
WHY?, BECAUSE
YOU'RE A POVVO
WHAT ON GOD'S
EARTH, ON TODA
EPISODE OF..., R
SISTER SHERRIE
HAVE A DAY OFF
GASP...STOP IT

LOVE

I'M TAKEN, YOU'RE SINGLE

think, of all the subjects in this book, love and relationships are the ones most changed by the Internet. Because love is more intimate than fashion or food, more hopeful than homes or holidays, and more personal than pets or products, it is most changed when pumped up on social media's serotonin steroids. It is the one that does the saddest impression of itself when performed for clicks.

Because love, like beauty, is in the eye of the beholder, but now the Internet makes it possible for your love to be projected and in the eyes of six million beholders, it changes everything. I'm sorry, Mr Shakespeare, but the course of true love *did* run smooth – I've seen it on Insta. John, Paul, bad news, money can not only buy me love but my love can *print* money, and will someone write another letter to the Corinthians, to let them know that love *does* now boast, and it *is* proud? St Paul didn't know about the hotties with tripods.

Humanity's most noble impulse gave birth to a cash cow, and the rest of us are chowing down on its sour milk.

Which shouldn't be a surprise. Love has been an effective sales technique for thousands of years. It has been used instrumentally by kings and queens, poets and playwrights – and that guy who came up with the idea of Valentine's Day. We should have seen it coming. We should have realised that if love can be used to buy kingdoms, get bums on seats and sell novelty cards, it can certainly

We should have realised that if love can be used to buy kingdoms, get bums on seats and sell novelty cards, it can certainly be used to sell itself (+ yoga mats).

be used to sell itself (+ yoga mats).

I think that is the problem, though, where the social media/love dynamic is stranger and more dangerous than any kind of entrepr*amore*ship that existed before it. Internet love sells itself and doesn't admit it. At least if some 12th-century king betrothed his 12-year-old daughter to a 46-year-old Viking in exchange for Jutland, he might have *admitted* that he was doing it for the feudal gains. He wouldn't have said, 'IDK, just thought it was cute', as he carted her off into the grizzled hands of Harold One Tooth.

The lies go deeper though. It's not just that Internet love sells itself, it sells A LOAD OF OTHER THINGS that it pretends are completely unrelated to the big free love bonanza that is front and centre. The Happy™ Internet couples don't directly monetise the love itself, only the searing sense of loneliness and inadequacy they create along with it. This is genius. This is like negging.[1] Because there is no more willing customer than a person who believes that they are currently unlovable and has been given private access to someone who has found the answer. There is no one more confused than a person who can't understand why they never get love (trust me). In this way, online love merchants are actually more like medieval plague doctors than salespeople – they see the confusion and prey on the lack of understanding people have. They have found a problem with no answer ('Why does no one love me?') and respond by saying, 'Not sure, but look how much someone loves ME... And buy my yoga mat.' Actually, again, on reflection, I prefer the plague doctor. At least they admit that they are *trying* to cure you, even if, like the romanstagrammer, they

---

[1] The deeply questionable practice of subtly insulting women to make them attracted to you. It is peddled by dating gurus who have clearly not succeeded with the more obvious option of being nice.

know they have absolutely no power to do so.

So, we've confirmed that people in Happy™ relationships on the Internet are actually worse than 12th-century child-traders and plague doctors (this disclaimer should now be algorithmically inserted into any post that contains a heart emoji, 'Brunch – heart – I would sell my daughter to One Tooth' type of thing), but we need to dig deeper into why. I think we need to start with some maths.

One influencer is a problem. Two unrelated influencers are two problems, twice as bad. Two influencers, together, filming themselves being in love, are actually the problem squared. They multiply the nonsense by at least itself, creating a far *bigger* problem because one person may be a fraud, but two or more is a conspiracy. The first conspiracy of the love influencers can simply be boiled down to, 'Who is holding the camera?' How are these people travelling the world and filming themselves from all manner of distances and in all manner of intimate situations with a *moving* camera? Well, I'll tell you. IT'S BECAUSE THERE IS A THIRD PERSON. THIS IS POLYAMORY. Or it's actually way more depressing. It's not polyamory, it's just that the millions of lonely people gorging themselves on lonely crisps are actually being represented in the moment by one lonely person who just follows a couple around the world videoing them. This person will necessarily be unloved and may possibly be a great character for a romcom. Hear me out.

Romcom idea. There are two influencer couples. They are absolute pilchards. Each couple has its own loveless camera servant who travels around with them – one guy, one girl (I would love for this idea to represent more diverse sexualities, but we're working[2] with *Hollywood* here, people). Both the influencer couples are not in love. It is all fake.[3] The camera people they have working for them are actually doing a great job of concocting the appearance of affection between the couples. They have never found love themselves, so have become really good at imagining what it must be like. Each evening, the camerapeople (who have not met!) spend long hours planning what the most romantic version of tomorrow would be like – at the pyramids, by a pool, in a glass room at the top of a very high building. They picture love in all its forms and make their influencers the most loved fake lovers the Internet has ever loved.

The two couples are rivals. Then the influencers start to grow apart. In both couples. They are going to break up, but they have one final plan: go to Paris to make the loveliest video and sell the most nonsense possible before they eventually break up and become singleness influencers. It is on this trip that all hell/heaven breaks loose.

During a long, lonely, love-planning session in a swoony Parisian café, the two camerapeople lock eyes across the room. He notices that she is crafting elegant, romantic hashtags that simultaneously express deep affection and sell moisturiser. She passes by a few times to take a look at his notepad as she goes to collect another coffee. He must be a fake love cameraperson as well, she thinks. On her last trip, she lingers a bit longer, uncertain whether to introduce herself, and sees that he's designing a caption for a picture by the river. 'Seine-timental snaps' is his working brief.

She stops, 'Fake love Insta by the river?'

He nods.

'Seine-timental won't land – the followers won't know

---

2 Imagining working.
3 Like most *Love Island* 'forever' romances levels of fake.

that river's name and they'll be too confused to buy the pointless stuff. How about something based on the lyrics of 'Moon River'… something about drifters travelling around the world… Then you can probably get an affiliate link for Booking.com in there too.'

She walks away. He grins.

They end up talking all night.

Anyway, long story short, the two camerapeople fall in love, but the TWO INFLUENCER COUPLES ACTUALLY SWAP PARTNERS AS WELL. It turns out that one of each couple likes surfing or something and the others are into knitting or whatever and they fall in love too. The film can end with the two influencer couples at the wedding of the camerapeople, taking pictures of *them*.

'Those are *not* going on socials!' the former camerawoman laughs.

Fade to black.

You stay to watch every credit (money's worth) and then google whether the actors and actresses in the couple are actually dating each other or they have a partner IRL, because you feel like you really know them. You find out who did the Korean subtitles and then the final credit rolls: 'Based on the ramblings of ShabazSays'. I have made it. You have made it. The world is a better place.

Or something like that.

I actually think it would be hard to make the fictional influencers quite as bad as the people who do this in reality – or, you know, something *like* reality. These couples go to Paris as a last hurrah, but there are genuine videos out there of people going on a surprise first date in Paris. First of all, LIES. But, second, if not lies, WHAT ARE YOU DOING, GIRL?! That is some Patrick Bateman *American Psycho* nonsense. If you are going on a first date with someone, always entertain the possibility that they might be an absolute menace (can you tell I'm not dating?) and, as a result, be in a place where you know the number for the police, have somewhere you can go, where you know… *anything*. Getting on a plane with a dude who is willing to pay $500 dollars to take you far, far away is a serious, serious drapeau rouge.[4] First, he is taking you far, far away (rouge). Second, he thinks that spending loads of money on you is a good way to make you like him (ROUGE). Third, IT'S PARIS ON YOUR FIRST DATE (ROUGE PLUS). If that is not a sign this guy is, like, a bit much, then I don't know what is. Are you gonna realise it's all a bit claustrophobic as you're flying to Venice for Date 2? When he builds you a Taj Mahal on Date 3? Or tries to propose on top of a giant sculpture of your face he made on Date 4? Don't wait until then – realise now. When he suggests Paris for your first date, run. Or post it all on Instagram so the authorities are aware of your movements.

I do wonder whether alerting authorities is actually a motivation for a lot of social media love. The idea is that you post everything in case the other person goes on a killing spree and then you have evidence. I look into the eyes of these people and I feel it is plausible. Take the videos that are filmed, in black and white, above someone's *literal* bed. You have probably seen them – they are like grainy CCTV footage (old-school *Big Brother* style) and they capture what a couple do while they are asleep. At some point in the night they might hug and that will be enough to generate plenty of desperate clicks. My question is, why do you have CCTV trained on your bed? That is so dark. What are you trying to

---

[4] Red flag.

find? Either you absolutely don't trust the one other person that sleeps in there or you are actually deranged enough to see the opportunities for good, candid sleep content. It's probably the second one, but that is just too much for my 90s brain to handle. Don't they know that there are loads of good love camerapeople out there? Why not just suspend them in a harness above your bed all night to capture content? That I could live with.

It's the lack of intimacy that kills me or, at least, the complete destruction of any genuine intimacy by the desperation to capture something that looks like it. Whatever happened to two people being closer with one another than anyone else in the world? Knowing things that no one else knows? Going places that no one else goes (I think I'm quoting Westlife now)?[5] If you are mining the bits where you are not conscious in the name of social clout, then what is there that is only yours? This is unlovable.

I think it is even more disappointing that, even with 24-hour CCTV footage of these relationships, there is a complete lack of conflict. No arguments, no disagreements and no 40-minute discussions of what to watch on Netflix. The relationships are all happy, all the time, and I feel this is setting quite a dangerous example. A generation of people are growing up and being led to believe that conflict is not part of a happy relationship.[6] This means that they will either shy away from any relationship that contains disagreement or become so ashamed of the conflict in their relationship

----

[5] Unless that means we have to pay some sort of royalty, in which case I am definitely just being poetic.
[6] Trust me, children form their ideas of romance early. I was raised on Bollywood and it still hurts that no one has expressed their love for me in the form of a choreographed 64-person dance routine.

that they hide it from the world and end up in situations that are genuinely unhealthy.

This is just one of the reasons, I think, that we need a campaign for social media literacy. I'm dead serious and this is the start. Children need to be taught how to spot a myth on the Internet. It is one thing for *adults* to decide that so much of what they see on socials is a weird, manipulative advert, but for kids who grow up on social media it is really hard not to have your world view distorted for ever. I actually started the ShabazSays page because of this (BTS CONTENT ALERT). I was working in a school and a lot of the kids were from families who were in very difficult financial circumstances. Many were on free school meals and many more were just above the threshold, so didn't even have that safety net. I noticed that these children were living a really hard life, but entertaining themselves by watching videos of people with pretend perfect lives. For them, both their poverty and their potential to soon be a cryptoking/ DubaiBossGirl (if they followed instructions or paid a monthly fee) were realities. Instead of being slowly introduced to the truth – that social mobility in the UK today is incredibly limited and that they would have to work very hard if they were to ever have more security than their parents could offer them – they believed there were two states of being: real-life poor and Internet rich, and the path between the two was short and sweet.

So I started making videos, trying to offer a bit of commentary on the world these kids were taking in. I wanted them to have a reality check. I don't know if I succeeded, but I do know that there is a lot more to be done. We all need to be reminded of what is true and what is performance in online culture and, in this instance, that means remembering social media relationships are no model for real-world ones. I know I'm preaching to the converted – you are probably the sort of person who does remind others of this, and I hope you do. If you are anything like the gang who gave me tips on how to date on the cheap, then

We all need to be reminded of what is true and what is performance in online culture and, in this instance, that means remembering social media relationships are no model for real-world ones.

you are probably doing it right now, fresh from a picnic date with the frugal love of your life and getting ready to picket a crypto conference.

Or you are like the many who sent in the first tip for dating on the cheap, which is **be single**. I know, this is a bit of a loophole in terms of dating, but I can tell you from experience, it works. Mathematical studies have shown that by simply reducing the number of people on a date from two to one, you can reduce costs and improve your mental state by up to 50 per cent! Now, that's what I call a saving. If you happen to be comparing mono-dating to polyamorous or polygamous situations, then the mono-date can actually lead to even greater results. Now I know some people think that, 'It's not really a date if you're on your own' (thanks, waiter) and that, 'We don't really need to put out a second plate and set of glasses if no one else is coming', but I think learning to love yourself and your single life is both cheap and empowering. If you are happy with friends and family and haven't found the right person, OWN IT. Two is not always better than one, even if it's harder to do a 'Romantic Proposal Video' by the Eiffel Tower if you have to play the one on your knees and edit in a picture of yourself receiving the ring.

I do genuinely believe that the single life is far better than a relationship which has not been built on good foundations, though, and definitely better than the ones which would come out of this suggestion I received: **Swipe right based on the average salary of people who have graduated from that institution** – that is, choose your partner based on their expected income. Now that is a strong povvo hustle, but it is too much for me. That is to love as loo roll stealing is to beauty, so I can't give it the seal of approval. In fact, in many ways I think this idea is the *opposite* of what we all agree is the povvo ethos: to not get caught up in appearances, to look deeper... to find deals. Choosing a partner because they might be rich is like following an account because their life seems perfect. It is superficial and it avoids the mucky, beautiful reality of being a povvo. So say no to sugar daddies, and no to high-fructose boyfriends.

The term 'sugar daddy' is pretty weird now I think of it. There is nothing sugary about these daddies. As a rule, when I think of sugar, I think of sweetness, and when I think of sweetness, I do not think of a sweaty 60-year-old man on his third marriage with four shirt buttons undone. Salt papi would work better, but that name is taken. Bitter uncle could work? 'I'm just trying to find me a Bitter Uncle girrrrrl' kind of captures it. Mostly it captures the facts that the relationship might not be tasty (bitter) and you may not like them very much (uncle), but they may be old and rich.

If you can find someone who is rich and generous who you actually like, great news. It is highly unlikely, though, and the only explanation for such a person existing is some sort of inherited wealth. As a person who got *all* of his inheritance at birth,[7] I appreciate that we shouldn't all be held accountable for what we are given by previous generations, so I am willing to let you date the lord or lady of your choice. Again, though, I don't think this should be a *focus* of your dating approach; it really should be a coincidence that they are also an heir to a biscuit fortune or their mum sold an interior design business to the Saudi royal family. If you go looking for it, then you are automatically setting your relationship on an uneven footing based on money.

I realise that these povvo tips are less do's and more don'ts at the moment, so I will focus on some genuinely useful ones. Such as **free dates**. No, I don't mean small, delicious dried fruits, I mean free excursions. These are political acts, because the idea that a date has to cost money and the more money it costs, the greater the romance involved, is a lie. I can only think this lie has its roots in some weird patriarchal idea that a man is starting the process of buying his future wife from the first date and the amount of money put into the dating process is like a modern dowry. It's weird and we should forget about it. If you can go on free dates and have a great time, then enjoy! Just remember to follow the Three Ps: **parks, picnics** and er... **perambulation**. OK, I know, 'perambulation' is a weird word, but I wanted a way to say 'go for walks' that started with a 'p'. Because going for walks is as free as it gets, it's fun and it's genuinely been proven to make for easier conversation.[8] (This is a genuine piece of research. I know I've done a lot of fake science so

---

[7] Inherited trauma. I intend to pass it down.
[8] Movement = focus + endorphins, while any awkwardness of constant eye contact is reduced because you are side by side. I recommend walking side by side. Do not walk a few paces behind.

far, but this one's true.)
Parks are great (or any
kind of generally green
area) because the open
spaces allow your eyes to
relax and being among
trees and natural features
does the same for your

❝ ❞

**So, by making your date
a walk in the park, you
can genuinely make your
date a walk in the park.**

mind. So, by making your date a walk in the park, you can genuinely make your date a walk in the park. You are not only saving coin but you are also getting a more relaxed experience with less of the awkwardness that can be the absolute killer of any date.

The picnic bit is where you can go to town (ironically, because you are doing the opposite of going to town). If you are packing the goods, then you can employ all of the good sense that you use around food (yellow stickers, price per kg, margarine tubs) and go out for a meal that doesn't cost the earth. Even better, you get to showcase some of your frugal cooking skills (Leftovers? NO, I ACTUALLY MADE THIS YESTERDAY FOR OUR DATE) and show some real, personal interest in what your date likes by chatting beforehand about what they like. Are you vegetarian? What kind of puds do you like? You prefer Aldi to Waitrose RIGHT? You can be the hero and save yourself an awkward moment over the bill at the end.

If you want to take your cheap and cheerful lovin' a step further, then you could PPP before going somewhere freefreefree because there are loads of free date spots out there. Free concerts. Free museums. Libraries. I know these things don't always scream 'great date', but I think it is mostly because we've all accepted the idea that if you don't get a panoramic video of your sushi on the observation deck of the Shard, then you're being short-changed. We have to alter that. We have to pioneer the library date (I know, this one is the hardest sell) and be willing to accept that, although we won't feel super bougie, we will get to know something more about the other person (Can they read? Do they own a library card? Do they run away from someone who suggests going for a date at a library?).

Another option, slightly above the completely free date, is the cheap one. This is a gold mine (FOR ALL THE GOLD YOU WILL SAVE) and there are lots of ways to go out with someone that don't involve a £30 per head bill (or more) at the end. Lots of people suggested **going for coffee** rather than a meal. This is clever as it gives you a bit of time to sus whether they are sus and decide if they are worth the price of an avocado toast. You also get to avoid any 'your place or mine' chatter if you are not looking for that, as it's probably the middle of the day. Best of all, you can pretend you have to leave because you have something pressing to do, which is a harder sell halfway through a dinner date. I do think this is a good option for a first date – a 'getting to know you' move – but if you want to go for something a bit more romantic, you could up the ante to **an ice cream date**. I loved this suggestion. Ice cream is just fun. It has a power that no one really understands. You go for ice cream and things are good because ice cream serves no other purpose than enjoyment. It's also perfect as you can combine it with perambulation, and *if you must*, take a nice photo that you can pretend is of the ice cream but is actually of your sweet little mittens holding cones. This is cute and makes my cynicism wither away. See, ice cream is amazing – it's frozen but it can still melt a cold heart.

I may be a cynic, but the line between shrewdness and cynicism is small, and that's why we love and trust one another here. Some seriously shrewd tips came in that I feel I have to just combine together into the perfect povvo date. So, hear me out. It's your third date. You've done the coffee and then the ice cream special. They went well. You like your date. Now you want to go to the next level, so follow this foolproof povvo plan from the gang. You start the day by **getting your hair done at a training salon.** Look, it's not always perfect, but it is *possible.* It is a salon. That is a great start. On your way to the date, you swing by Boots or Walgreens (hello, again, US folk) to **get free perfume spritzes and ALL your make-up done (samples).** This is extra effective as we all know that perfume doesn't last, so getting a spritz on the way in will maximise its impact. It's a Wednesday, so **two-for-one cinema** tickets are a must. The film should be something easy enough, not basic, but not a high-concept foreign language flick. You want things to talk about afterwards but, equally, you don't want to have spent an hour crying in front of your future husband/wife. Now you are off for dinner. Find somewhere small and cheap by **researching the menu before you go.** Now here is where we separate the elite povvos from the rest. You choreograph a **fake engagement to get free drinks.** Look, don't judge me, you are either up for it or you are not, but there are some of us who are willing to spread false joy and lies into the world in exchange for freebies (see we're not that different from influencers really). You've eaten well and said no to dessert. The bill has been reasonable because the drinks were free and you were still quite full from the snacks you snuck into the cinema. You wouldn't mind something sweet, though, so you **pretend it is your birthday for a free Krispy Kreme.** Both of you. Pretend you share a birthday.

Because if you sign up to the Krispy Kreme app, you get a free doughnut on your birthday and you also get to pretend you and your date are some sort of romantic twins. Dreamy.

Obviously, after this date, you are going to be inseparable and have enough money left over to put down a deposit on a house together. The two of you are now in it for the long haul but, don't worry, the cheap romance doesn't need to end there. Our povvos have lots of handy recommendations for staying on the right side of the bailiffs even after you have found love. It has been suggested that you **find someone sleepy**. This would have been useful to find out *before* you started dating and I'm not sure people really share information about their sleepyness on dating apps, but I do agree that it is a great way to make savings. The same can be said for the suggestion to **date an introvert.** As a rule, I find extroverts to be more expensive than introverts – we run hot and tend to make the sort of impulsive decisions that leave us all poorer. So try to find a sleepy introvert and make sure to **tell them you hate expensive things.** This stops you from getting into that silly gifts nuclear arms race that couples have, where one person gets an expensive gift and then the other has to top it, over and over again, until you both have lots of really nice candles, but no money left.

I've seen this loads of times – the kind of gift one-upmanship where each person is wondering if their gift is as good/as expensive as the one their partner got them last time. Free yourself and judge gifts by their usefulness rather than their price because **loving gifts are things people need.** I know this may bring up bad memories of Christmas socks and birthday stationery, but you're a grown-up now and you need a chopping board so feel the love. Yes, it is hard to get excited about that 10-year anniversary toothbrush holder at first, but remember that, in a way, your partner is not just trying to help you hold toothbrushes, they are holding *you*, because they know it's what you need. You also get to have upright toothbrushes, which is way more hygienic, and then, by your 20th anniversary, you may even be able to stretch to a freestanding electric toothbrush. That's love. Those are gifts that keep on giving, the ones that you keep on using and keep you saving.

Honestly, all this talk of frugal first love is restoring my faith in romance itself. Unlike the love that we are shown on social media, it doesn't seem magical or impossible, perfect or otherworldly. It feels real, like something I could have, when someone will have me. The romance of povvos is real, it does not boast and it is not proud, and money literally can't buy it (only deals). It is a return to true love, budget, slightly bonkers and beautiful.

Because beauty, like love, is in the eye of the toothbrush holder.

BEG YOUR PARI
ROUND BALLY IC
RICH, YOU'RE PO
SPOKEN LIKE A
POVVO, BECAUS
IOT AN ANIMAL
VHY?, BECAUSE
OU'RE A POVVO
VHAT ON GOD'S
ARTH, ON TODA
PISODE OF..., RC
SISTER SHERRIE
IAVE A DAY OFF
GASP. STOP IT I

FASHION

'I GOT MY FIRST PAIR OF LOUBOUTINS WHEN I GRADUATED HIGH SCHOOL'

got a bit sentimental in the previous chapter. It was a rollercoaster ride. I went from being outraged that THEY'VE[1] RUINED LOVE, to feeling intense loneliness on behalf of third-wheeling camerapeople, before eventually becoming dewy-eyed at all the ways you lovebugs scuttle around the pitfalls of the cost of loving[2] crisis. I had some serious feelings about a serious subject.

So, in the name of fairness, I'm going to share some unserious feelings about a genuinely unserious subject. Fashion. And by 'fashion', I don't mean the efforts of many very brilliant people working in this industry and making great strides when it comes to fashioning (ahem) a more inclusive, sustainable variety of this. I'm talking about the very (incredibly skinny) bones of certain aspects of 'high fashion'. If I was outraged about how far the Internet has dragged love from its lovely origins, then I have to give fashion some credit. In many senses, it was always nonsense, so it is only nonsense with a megaphone now that social media has got involved. Yes, it's making more money than ever. Yes, the high-end 'houses' can dress sickly models up as sort of goth gimps, walk them around a muddy field and make billions/art, but that's nothing new. Fashion was really always just rich people finding a way to wear their money and call it something else. This particular segment of fashion was always ridiculous because it was always just clothes and the performance of clothes.

Now, I don't have any beef with 'Just Clothes'. I wear 'Just Clothes' (yes, I know, shock horror, 'Shabaz Leaves Onesie Scandal!'). Clothes are great, I'd feel naked without

---

[1] You know, them.
[2] Copyrighted. I don't know the process for copyrighting a phrase, but I want it, so consider this my claim.

them. They are the difference between nudity and normality, between flashing and dashing, being ogled and being *seen*, but 'high fashion', well it's just a load of abnormal flash folks going out on the ogle. So I congratulate you, high fashion, on being as weird as social media before social media even existed. You created the blueprint for beautiful people with blank expressions doing weird stuff to make other rich people feel happy and everyone else sad. High fashion, you were fashion before it was fashionable.

So, yeah that's it really. Love you, high fashion. You're the best.

Lol jk. You are still the worst, and the ways social media has given you a platform to normalise your carefully crafted abnormality are beyond the pale (and pale, pale models). But, again, disclaimer: if *you* work in fashion, if you're a designer or a model or even an Internet show-off, I want you to know that I don't think *you* are the worst. I don't feel strong emotions about the individuals in any of the businesses I describe throughout this book. (Even the love influencers. Yes, I know, I said they are worse than the child-trader and plague-doctors.) What I *do* feel strongly about are the industries and cultures that grow up around things like fashion and food – the vibes and the business models, and the business of models is no different.

So, people working in fashion, I want you to know, I respect you. Models, designers and marketers have a job to do, and I don't hate, you wanna make a living. It's just that together, and without any sort of agreement, these individuals have become an industry – in this case, one so clueless that it genuinely doesn't even cringe when Bella Hadid says, 'I never, growing up, had anything designer. My mom wouldn't let me. I think I got my first pair of Louboutins when I graduated high school' (Ehis, 2021). An industry that can't admit it is just selling clothes. Like Topman or ASOS. Which sort of makes me feel sorry for the high-fashion industry. It spends all its days just making clothes but can never admit that they are just clothes. If it did, then the whole thing would just fall apart, as you can't admit that you are basically Topman and still charge thousands. You are like an emperor who can't be told the truth, who lives a life of incredible wealth that is only possible because of an incredible lack of self-awareness. The high-fashion industry is its own emperor, like in the story, but, on the upside, it makes everyone need new clothes.

I actually feel like if the emperor from *The Emperor's New Clothes* started an Instagram fashion channel, it would pop off. The emperor would be rich and naked (two very saleable assets on the Internet) and unbox expensive-looking packages of nothing. (What is as exclusive as nothing? 'This is the best nothing, you just don't get it'.) Unboxing nothingness is a powerful metaphor for the whole Internet high-fashion performance. In fact, unboxing in general leaves a lot to unpack.[3] For anyone who is analogue enough to not know what the unboxing industry involves, basically, just picture someone getting something and opening it. Then, depending on the excitement they can

Unboxing nothingness is a powerful metaphor for the whole Internet high fashion performance. In fact, unboxing in general leaves a lot to unpack.

---

[3] Snort, snort.

create around this process or the exclusivity of the box they open, they make loads of money. It is a diverse field, pioneered by small children with YouTube channels. It started with toys and then became a fashionable pursuit. Unboxing videos are popular because they give people a sort of consumer contact high. Seeing someone open something they've bought[4] offers a homeopathic[5] version of buying and opening something yourself. If you are addicted to online shopping, then unboxing offers a small hit of the dopamine that you get from buying things yourself, with less of the regret when it's rubbish, but more frustration if it is really good.

In my (sometimes) humble opinion, unboxing is the jumping-off point for all Internet high fashion. It is the move that let the cat out of the bag (do not watch videos where there are actual cats in the bag) and a great example of how everything about fashion on the Internet is about feelings and not clothes. Unboxing is about hope, expectation and release. Like gambling, you are very unlikely to win, but there is always another chance to play. If it were about the clothes, then people would just look up expensive bags on brands' websites, but unboxing is closer to a magic trick than a product list. It uses the same energy as a circus magician who brings a beautiful assistant back after they've made them invisible. TAP THE HERMÈS BAG-BAG THREE TIMES AND SAY THE MAGIC WORD. And, poof. A bag comes out of the bag. Sweet relief. It's quite nice. It's quite a nice bag. Hurray. The magic trick always works, and it's equal opportunities because you don't need to actually spend your teenage years practising magic to

---

4 Been gifted.
5 Watered down to one part in a million.

be able to do it. You just need to inherit money and have parents who consider unboxing to be a proper career. It's nice work if you can get it.

It is also very important for the relationship between brands and social media. I don't think I would actually even know the names of luxury brands if people weren't doing unboxing magic tricks with French 'fashion houses' online. The partnership seems to be working well, though. Fashion and socials go together like peaches and cream or fish and chips, while being as useful as a chocolate teapot.[6] Again, it's our old friend 'exclusivity' that makes this all possible. When we, normal people, own clothes, it's not the fact that you have something that makes it worthwhile, it's whether you like it and whether other people agree that it looks nice on you. That is why all the things fashion is supposed to care about – like the cut, colour palettes and designs – are important when it comes to actual clothes. They will look different on different-looking people and that's great. Simply owning something that your friend doesn't have is of zero benefit to your or their life. When you introduce social media, though, simply owning something that other people can't have is somehow an asset. It is a business model based on the same principles as a five-year-old going, 'Na-na-na-na-naaa-na you can't have this'. Except that, instead of this creating one other sad five-year-old, it creates 270,000 likes from people who (I can only assume) actually enjoy being tormented like a child.

I just looked up the most successful fashion brands on

---

[6] I actually keep accidentally making up bad influencer videos. 'Come and See my Chocolate Teapot' would get so many likes. You make the tea but you sort of end up with hot chocolate. IDK.

social media (yeah, I research). Apparently, Burberry is particularly good at social media marketing (Spillane, 2023). No shock there. When you have a business that, from what I can see, historically was about making scarves for rich grandmothers and you transition to become a youth brand, you've done something well. No, the bit that surprised me is that one of the great things they have done is create a game called Blankos Block Party, which also houses limited edition NFTs by Burberry (Burberry, 2022). First of all, a *video* game. A *Burberry* video game? Have a day off. I imagine the point of this game is to level up by generating irrational jealousy in the poor with your toolbox of exclusive checked things, but I'm not going to even give it a thought. Second, 'limited edition NFTs'. I would rather not get started on NFTs[7] because they are so stupid they make me want to become non-fungible, but 'limited edition'? Isn't the whole point of NFTs that they are unique (and absurd)? Aren't they defined by being limited? Do you really need to make unique, imaginary items 'limited editions'? Does a load of code, which is nothing if not a digital representation of exclusivity, have to be made *somehow more exclusive* by being called limited edition? HURRY UP, GUYS, THEY'RE GONNA RUN OUT.[8] I wonder whether I have actually missed a trick here by not making this book a 'limited edition'. If celebrities can make their billion-dollar companies with 10,000 sweatshop labourers fail to produce enough lip kits in the name of exclusivity, maybe I can too.

Apparently, Burberry is also great because it created something called #theartofthetrench, a community where users

---

7 I think it stands for 'Nice F'in Try'.
8 But also WHAT IS FUNGIBLE?

could upload photographs of themselves wearing Burberry trenches. Sorry, Burbs, but you haven't actually created anything there. That's what used to be called a photo album, now gets called 'an Instagram' and should *never* be called 'a community'. That's an insult to communities everywhere.

I just did some more research (I'm getting into it). Apparently, according to an article in *Vogue* (Maguire, 2022), 'TikTok unboxing is luxury fashion's low-cost marketing tool'. No schnitzel schnerlock. Unboxing and social media advertising is a way for very powerful brands to do lots of very effective advertising for very little money. How does this work and where are the margins? In our eyes. Companies used to pay to make us look at things we weren't gonna buy; now we pay with our time and they get a cut. It's genius. Anyway, everyone in this article seems to think unboxing is a really good thing and they share their reasons for this after what I think is one of the saddest opening paragraphs I have ever read (Maguire, 2022):

Back in March 2020, Audrey Peters started out on TikTok like many others, posting comedy videos. Her content comprised witty sendups of New York boroughs and hotspots, a concept that eventually ran out of steam. She first experimented with a luxury unboxing video in March this year following a shopping trip to Italy. It garnered 1 million views, she recalls. 'Now unboxing content is my best-performing content on TikTok,' she says. 'So, I ran with it.' Since June, her views have pushed up by 160 per cent, with engagement up 140 per cent. Her profile has 37.2 likes.

It seems to me that this story speaks volumes about the whole unboxing thing. People, consciously or unconsciously, or for the likes, decide that their personality and creativity is less interesting to the world than opening boxes. It is something akin to saying, 'I love art and wanted to share my watercolours with the world, but then, one day, on a trip back from the shops, I realised that I had left my webcam on a white wall I had been painting and gained loads of followers. People just seem to prefer watching paint dry.'

From where I'm sitting (read: lying in bed), I feel like this was presented as an empowering story. It also involved a shopping trip from New York to Italy. Not a trip to the shops, like down the road in your dressing gown, but to another continent, to go shopping. It takes hard work and talent to make it in this game, but if you can travel across the world to buy bags and take videos of those bags coming out of other bags, you might just be able to make it, kid.

If you are not rich enough already to invest in holiday handbag content (WHAT IS WRONG WITH YOU?) then you have two options: you can either take out loans to buy expensive high-end designer handbags or you can take out smaller loans to cover the less expensive things that you buy out of shame after watching someone else opening boxes with high-end designer handbags inside. It is important to remember that if you choose the first option, you don't actually have to go to Italy or France to do your shopping. You can just pretend. No one knows if the bag came from a shop in Milan or Manchester or even the Internet, so you can save £100 on the air fare when buying your £10,000 bag. It's a small saving, but it may be the difference between profit and loss, and this *is* a business.

It is a business that, all joking aside, does actually create quite serious problems. Social media envy, shopping addiction and 'shop now, pay later' financing are a recipe for serious debt traps and people are genuinely sacrificing their needs in the name of their wants, which have been relentlessly pushed on them. In their book *The Spirit Level: Why Equality is Better for Everyone*, Kate Pickett and Richard Wilkinson (2010), who study the factors affecting health and disease, argue that inequality is the driving force behind far more social problems than we realise, because the experience of having little and spending time looking at people who have a lot makes you more likely to sacrifice things like nutrition, health and social interactions in the name of buying things to look less poor. I think this describes the danger of social media high fashion quite well. If you normalise people owning £10,000 bags, you will feel abnormal, and if you feel abnormal because you cannot buy pointless, expensive things, you will be far more likely to buy pointless, cheaper things to feel better. If you are already in a situation where you have limited money, then that will mean giving up on important things or building up debt.

This is an awful thing, but it is also a part of what is funding the massive profits of luxury brands that have found this to be a 'low-cost marketing tool'. It is a low cost for them, but it can be a high cost for ordinary people. There is also a high cost to the less ordinary people who can genuinely afford a bag for £10,000. That cost, again, is £10,000. For a bag. A supposedly practical but also non-essential item of clothing.

Bags have become the show-off item of choice for a few reasons, but the fact that they are not actually clothing is one of them. You don't need a bag to be clothed so, really, it is the cherry on top of any show-off's outfit. In a time when dressing expensively seems to require wearing really simple beige things that only other rich people can tell are very expensive, the bag is the one part of the outfit where you can signal your wealth to the povvos. Povvos know bags. We know hessian bags, rucksacks and bog-standard blue, corner shop bags that are not capable of carrying anything more than two Freddo bars[9] and a pack of Discos crisps. So the bag speaks a language we understand, and it is visible from the distance at which we are allowed to stand and watch. It makes sense, because, although Gwyneth Paltrow isn't gonna let this povvo see the label on her cashmere, I'll be able to make out Kim K's handbag from the 6-metre distance that her minders would demand. This is why the expensive handbag has to be garish (visibility) and look very 1980s Trump sort of glamorous (visibility). In my eyes, all expensive bags look like counterfeits and all expensive bags could be replaced by signs that say, 'I'm rich, you're poor', with a bag for life superglued to the back to actually carry things. This would genuinely fulfil all the functions of an expensive super-bag, which are (1) carrying things and (2) generating loathing. They could even come in lots of varieties, so the people who like to have 30 different ones could still be satisfied. One sign could say, 'I'm rich', but others could say, 'Get out of my way, you povvo' or 'It's pronounced errrrr-mez.'

We would obviously need to organise it so that the sign could be written up in front of the buyer by a sales assistant, because, apparently, the personal touch is key to the luxury market. This emphasis on the 'personal touch' is slightly odd, though, because I would say that repeatedly meeting a person on a low to normal salary who hates you is the opposite of a close personal relationship but, somehow, having a short-term servant thrown into the package when buying a bag seems to

---

[9] Have you seen the inflation on them? Now, back in my day... No, I can't even be that guy.

be an essential part of the buying experience. It might be that the lives of the super-rich are actually so lonely that these interactions with customer service assistants are genuinely some of the most authentic experiences they have, and this makes me feel a bit sorry for them and a little less bad about my rucksack. I didn't need to pay extra for the person at the checkout at B&M to be my friend.

When it comes to the ways that the rest of us buy clothes, we actually do the opposite. We pay less and try not to think about the social impacts of the things we buy. I'm talking about the two F's. No, not *The Fast and the Furious*, but fast fashion, although some people *are* furious about it. I would imagine that fast fashion may split this room, with most against. I fall into the against camp, but I can see the argument that it is always the povvos who end up getting blamed when we're just buying the only things we can afford. The fashion industry bombards us with adverts to buy things, ramps up our jealousy using 'low-cost marketing tools' and then *we* get told off for buying what we can. *I WOULD HAVE SLOW FASHION IF I COULD AFFORD IT*, is a fair argument. So, if that's your take, I'll give you this much: it's not your fault. The world wants you to buy everything and you bought a £6 maxi dress, which is not the worst thing. But we povvos are shrewd, so we have to hold ourselves to higher standards and those standards are those of grandmothers.

Because, deep down, we know that we don't need to buy new clothes very often. We are just made to feel like absolute pond-dwellers because we can't. As proud povvos, though, we need to be strong, to know that all the marketing in the world can't take away our value and all the new T-shirts wouldn't make us any more worthwhile than we already are. Refusing to play their game and not allowing ourselves to be manipulated is the mark of true povvos. We know we can do it, because the grannies can, and the grannies give us strength. I recommend turning to a granny whenever there is a temptation to buy pointless stuff. Ask them

Deep down, we know that we don't need to buy new clothes very often. We are just made to feel like absolute pond-dwellers because we can't.

how often they buy new clothes. Find out how many maxi dresses they have. Tell them that some people buy new stuff every week. Their complete disgust should be enough to make you feel sane again. And, after you've heard how they saved up for six months in 1946 for some ladies' winklepickers, your perspective will be restored.

They may also teach you to **sew your own clothes,** which would be useful. This was a suggestion that came in from povvos a few times, and there's no denying it is a peak shrewd povvo move. Having skills that allow us to avoid manipulation by influencers and marketing is what we are all about. If you can sew, you can be like Marge Simpson with her one Chanel suit that she wore in multiple ways and became an estate agent. You can make hand-me-downs feel like pick-me-ups, and you can save money along the way because I know you already have that biscuit tin filled with sewing equipment somewhere. Of course, it will take time to get to the grandmother level of sewing, so if you need to get your fixing-fix sooner, instead, you could try **putting a drop of clear nail varnish on tights to stop runs from getting worse.** This is science, closer to magic if you ask me and satisfying as you'll be taking back from the beauty *and* fashion industries using guerrilla tactics. If you have ripped clothes that are sturdier than your average tights (or pantyhose for my American friends, although I really recommend you guys have a look at that word, it's just weird), then, of course, you can turn to our old friend **the safety pin**. A well-placed safety pin is fashion in its own right, just ask Vivienne Westwood, and if you really wear it with confidence, you can pretend that any safety pin was intentional and put there by the designer. Yes, I know it is a silk dress, but it's a *punk* silk dress. Maybe in the case of a silk dress, you should use **iron-on hemming tape,** as some community members have suggested, because they don't want to look like Johnny Rotten on their sister's wedding day.

These are all proper hacky hacks. They are artful dodges, Oliver twists in the tale of your relationship with consumerism, but there are some povvo hacks that don't even require a box of pins or tape. Some are as simple as **being Northern**[10] **to save on coats.** This idea, of Northern-ness as a state of mind, could actually really benefit the YouTube self-improvement psychobabble community. Rather than thinking like a CEO or a marine or a stoic, you should just be more Northern. Feeling cold? Think Northern. Disappointed about 40 years of underinvestment and failed industrial policies? (YOU KNOW YOU'VE BEEN THERE.) Be more Northern. It's about hardiness, an unwillingness to be broken by the merciless march of modernity, a willingness not to be everyone's cup of (very strong) tea. To avoid winter shopping, for ever. Coats are a Southern conspiracy, and if you conjure up your spirit animal (a 17-year-old girl on a night out in

---

[10] For my American friends, behave like those from the north of England, where it is colder.

Carlisle), you will be able to brave even the coldest temperatures with very little on.[11]

I have seen an alternative version of this put forward, which is, 'put on weight to save on coats' and, while I see the appeal, it can't quite get my Bad Housekeeping seal of approval. The problem is that you might have to buy other clothes as a result and just being more Northern is simpler. The alternative option, to 'never put on weight and keep wearing things for ever' also has too many issues attached. I already beat myself up when I put on weight (wrong, I know) and if I was to feel like each pound was making me poorer as well, I might just give up, so I'm gonna keep that out of the top tips. If you are naturally slim, though, I will haunt you if you ever buy new clothes.

I guess the downside of not changing shape is that you never get the experience of stealing clothes from a variety of siblings. **Borrow from your sibling** was a recurring theme in suggestions for this chapter, and there is nothing sweeter than realising you are now the perfect size to ~~steal~~ borrow clothes from another one. So see that as your prize for fluctuating in size. It is one of life's great joys – thrifty and shifty, and with the potential to launch a sibling disagreement that can last upwards of 50 years. Remember those winklepickers Grandma bought in 1946? There's still an argument going on about who wore them to the Trades Union dance and who wouldn't be proud to have an argument that outlasted the Cold War? In my house, we have resorted to literally labelling everything.

An advantage to staying in the same ballpark of weight

---

[11] I remember my first time going out down South and discovering that there was a thing called a cloakroom. For coats. I'd never seen the like.

is that it allows you to **wear the same item of fancy dress for ever.** I loved this one. Not just because I pictured a woman going to parties for 40 years dressed as a lobster but also because there is something so strong about it. It conveys an identity. She *is* The Lobster, and if you can be the lobster, then be The Lobster. All it requires is some foresight when deciding on your fancy dress life partner. Sexy maids or 'that kid from the Netflix show' aren't going to necessarily work in 2046, but lobsters should last (climate crisis pending). Just picture your funeral now (I do, often, and we are yet to confirm whether that is really healthy or really not) and some distant great-nephew with his new wife. See her face as it gradually dawns on her that in every other picture, you are dressed as a lobster. Watch as she weighs up whether it is rude to ask why or whether it is ruder that she doesn't already know all about his great-aunt's lobster thing. This should be motivation enough.

For some of you, this may feel a bit extreme. You just wanted to save some money on clothes, not become known across three counties as the lobster lady, so I will forgive you if you decide that you just want some more traditional thrifty options. These I will reel off pretty quickly. **Always wait for the sale.** I know, *Basic budget stuff, Baz,* but some people need to know this. There will always be a sale, and when it comes to clothes sales, it actually does make sense. They have these things called 'seasons' (which I will not acknowledge due to my commitment to being Northern) and 'seasons' mean sales. Simple. What I do not understand is why someone smarter, more driven and technologically savvy than me has not created an app or website where you can plug in all the clothes you want and it monitors the whole Internet for when they go on sale. Then notifies us.

This would be great and if I had the skill or supercomputers, I would make this my first venture. Unfortunately, I have neither, but I do have the knowledge that **old clothes become nightclothes become cleaning rags** and this is close enough to creating a billion-dollar tech company in my eyes. Why? Because I never have to buy nightclothes or cleaning rags, and I don't have to mingle with tech bros or venture capitalists because of it. It's a fair trade-off. You also get the nice memories that accompany your well-worn clothes whenever you have to scrub the floor, so it's a bit like being haunted by the friendly ghosts of clothes past. *Hi, NYE 2014 top, happy 2023, remember when we were young?* sort of thing. It's sweet. If it makes you sad, though, you can dress up as a lobster while you do it. Because lobsters are for ever.

It's why you never see lobster costumes in **second-hand shops.** I bet you're wondering if you have now and I know you haven't. Second-hand shops are great, but they don't get my lobster. Lobsters don't have hands.

The best thing about thrift shops is that you get to go on a treasure hunt and a shopping trip all at once. For the price of a second-hand item, you get a day out and the sense that you are a super sleuth, finding the deals that no one else could see. It's a bit like being an archaeologist, just instead of getting cursed by an Egyptian, you get welcomed by a volunteer called Pam, which is way nicer. If you are really operating at a high level of second-handing, you will have worked out where the best shop is in a wealthier area, and this means you not only feel like an archaeologist but a tourist as well. In my experience, it's a bit like getting one of those maps in LA that shows you to 'the homes of the stars' (I've never been), but instead you are touring the blouses of the upper middle class. It's a wild ride, and you don't actually have to buy anything, but you still get to find out that, only a few miles down the road, everyone is buying things from Karen Millen.

You, too, could buy things from Karen Millen one day. If you just dream hard enough, save long enough and then marry someone wealthy enough. The only problem is that the rich people you'd want to marry probably expect

❝❞

But remember that your self-worth should never be tied to the things you wear. Don't buy clothes to make yourself feel better and never feel worse about yourself because you can't wear something that the fashion industry has made you want.

you to already be wearing Karen Millen, not a lobster costume with loads of safety pins and clear nail varnish on it. So forget about them. Just buy it yourself and make sure you **apply the mother's discount.** The name might make it sound better than it is, like you are actually saving some money. In fact, the mother's discount is just the price you tell your mother[12] something cost when she asks how much it was. It is essential that you only tell her the discounted price[13] because, even after doing the maths, she will still be flabbergasted. (*Wait till I tell Grandma!* You can't, Grandma's off feuding with her sister about a top from 1953.) When you see her shock, you will either stick your heels in (**go for**

---

[12] Or another appropriate older person in your life.
[13] Remember to be careful with your calculations, though, because the mother will know you're lying if you say that an iPhone cost £50.

metal ones, they never wear down) or return the dress to Karen Millen. So **always keep the receipt.**

But remember that your self-worth should never be tied to the things you wear. Don't buy clothes to make yourself feel better and never feel worse about yourself because you can't wear something that the fashion industry has made you want. To do that is to take a deeply unserious subject too seriously. The greatest antidote to the manipulation that brands and social media marketers engage us in is a solid sense of self, and of our worth. Remember, they are just clothes, whatever brand they are, and that you are just great, however you are.

Particularly if you are dressed as a lobster.

BEG YOUR PAR[D]

[G]ROUND BALLY IC

[R]RICH, YOU'RE PO

[S]POKEN LIKE A

POVVO, BECAUS[E]

[N]OT AN ANIMAL

[W]HY?, BECAUSE

[Y]OU'RE A POVVO

[W]HAT ON GOD'S

[E]ARTH, ON TODA[Y]

[E]PISODE OF..., R[O]

[S]ISTER SHERRIE

[H]AVE A DAY OFF

[G]ASP, STOP IT

HOMES

LET ME SHOW YOU MY CAT LIFT

The National Trust was established in 1895 to conserve Great Britain's[1] historic buildings.[2] Its aim was to protect these timeless structures and preserve them for generations to come, so that people from all over the world could marvel at their stately grandeur. Unfortunately, not one of the buildings that the National Trust protects has a cat lift or candle pantry. As a result, I can only assume that the Trust has been beset by complaints from chronically online visitors who doubt whether the lords and ladies were actually even rich. '*I've* never seen the First Marquess Curzon of Kedleston post a video of his closet, so does he even count?' asked one disappointed visitor. 'I don't care about your house, Lady Dundas, I want to see your dog's "man cave"' added another.

This is evidence that we are at a historical peak of show-off culture. So I must speak. First, the show-offs came for the povvos and I said something, for I am a povvo. Then they came for the middle classes, and I said nothing, because, give over, you're doing all right, so stop moaning. Then the Internet came for our historical influencers, the great rich men and women who built[3] this country, and I could remain silent no longer... because I had to laugh. Yes, you heard it here first (because I made it all up), people who video their amazing and unnecessary houses are no longer just creating envy in the poor and living but also shaming the rich and the dead. 'I *know* you funded this ballroom with the proceeds of the famine in Bengal or whatever, Your Lordship, but if you didn't post it on Insta, did it even really happen? And where is the beige?'

---

[1] Scotland has its own one.
[2] And lots of other stuff.
[3] With the help of 500 million colonial subjects and 12-year-old Lancastrians working in the mills.

It truly is an achievement that 'I'm rich, you're poor' is more relevant now than it was in 1895. It makes me grateful to be alive right now, when wealthy people's cats have their own maisonettes and newborn babies can genuinely be more asset-rich than me (to be fair, one onesie is all it takes). It makes my job easier. While I would like to believe that Victorian Shabaz would have been able to throw some shade through the smog, I'm just not sure my jibes would land. The viscounts of the time of the Raj were more subtle than the homefluencers of social media and my page (it would have been a literal page, which I handed out among the villagers), just wouldn't have been popping. At least rich people used to *know* that it was annoying when people told you how great their house was – that's why they only let the povvos in after they were done with it.

Now we live in a time where showing off your home is a right, a privilege, even a career. The revolution might not be televised but the oligarchy is coming to a screen near you, all the time. This would probably shock and amaze history's rich folk. If you showed Instagram to some 19th-century barons, they'd be pulling their hair out, shouting, 'Don't SHOW it all to them! They're not supposed to *know*!' Rich people have always been aware that if they annoy us enough by dangling beautiful things in our faces, we'll have a revolution.[4] If we wanted to take that cat's lift we could and, unlike the landed gentry, homefluencers don't seem to be concerned about keeping us out and keeping us happy – they just want to video their cat going up and down.

Or maybe they have just found a more subtle approach.

---

4 The phrase 'money can't buy happiness' probably came out of a PR stunt run by the British. aristocracy after the French Revolution.

Whereas the robber barons of history built tiny schools for kids to go to on their days off from the mine, their contemporary equivalents have found smarter ways to keep us from revolting (yes, we are revolting, but we haven't *revolted*). Instead of throwing us a party once a year or creating poorhouses, they keep us in the loop by just *showing* us their rich houses. This means that the povvos and their pitchforks never actually rise up and demand equality, because we feel like we're being allowed in. They *let* us take a look round.

I got to see a jacuzzi on my phone. We all share here. We're equals.

So, fair play to them, they have kept the revolution at arm's length, while most of us exist in rooms where literally everything is at arm's length. My living room doesn't have enough space to swing a cat, while rich people's cats have *swinging* living rooms, but because they let us see inside, we feel *involved*.

I would like to be involved in a mortgage, thanks. I would like the property ladder to be more than just a device that helps me peer over the Internet's walls and see rich people's pantries. An Englishman's home may be his castle, but just showing me your castle doesn't help this Englishman come any closer to owning a home.

If you are questioning whether these millionaires are really having an impact on my ability to stump up for a two-up, two-down in Blackburn, I have to say, yes, there are knock-on effects. Property and, in particular, property in the UK, has become a global asset, a tradeable resource and a plaything. All the terrible industries in which the UK has been a world leader (tax evasion, fossil fuels, mining) have made a lot of people around the world rich, and those people have decided that the super-expensive houses in the UK we get to see on our phones are a great way to store their petrodollars. That means our old friends 'the gentry' now don't live in castles, just big, bland, beige houses. The people who lived in the big houses now live in the small ones. The people who used to be able to buy the small houses now rent flats, and me... well, I live at my mum's.[5]

It's called economics and, although I don't understand it, I've started ranting about it and that makes me feel like I do. And ranting is nine-tenths of the law. Or was it possession? Either way, I feel possessed when I look at the bad houses of social media. With rage. *Why*, you ask? Well, to start with – and this is not my most intellectually astute observation – they are just all so *bad*. How

How can you genuinely have unlimited money to spend on your house and make it look so bang average? Why are they all beige? Why are they all the same?

can you genuinely have unlimited money to spend on your house and make it look so bang average? Why are they all beige? Why are they all the same? I can only assume it is a tactic by interior designers and homewares companies to rinse more cash out of foolish milli-very-vanilli-billi-onaires. Here's my theory: if they make your house look fundamentally the same as the other rich people's houses, then you will

---

[5] And the Tories sold off many many council houses in the Right to Buy scheme.

have to mark out your territory somehow. Question 1: if Kim has a big, beige house and Kourtney does, too, how does K3 make her big, beige house stand out? (6 marks). Answer: by filling it with pointless, *expensive* nonsense. You see, the margins on nonsense items can be more... well, nonsensical, and that means the people behind the home decor can make more money. Whereas before, designers had to think about creating a unique space, using things like materials, colour and architecture, now they can make a unique space by introducing a tiny functioning kitchen for people's pets. This means that they don't have to do any actual designing, they can reuse the materials and leave with a cut of the tiny functioning pet kitchen hustle.

It's the only way I can make sense of it because it can't be that rich people only like beige. It can't be that the richer you get, the less capable you are of processing colour. There has to be some profit motive because I was led to believe that the whole thing about being rich is being able to have things which are unique, personalised, *couture*. Poor people live in terraced houses that look the same and rich people get to create bonkers mahogany ghost mansions in waiting because they want to really get a head start and practise their haunting in anticipation of the possibility they will have a great-granddaughter who marries a person of colour. Now it's all upside down. Being garish is poor; being expensively beige (while owning some manic tat) is rich. This is an insult to the opulent emperors of the past, the ones who, I've decided, I prefer to our modern emperors of the Internet. If Shabaz Says had been in operation during the reign of Nero or Gilgamesh or whomever, I would have been rooting for the big guy. Those emperors liked a bit of glam. Tutankhamun was a hun (as in Gemma Collins, leopard print, Chardonnay).

Atilla was literally a hun, but I'd like to believe his yurt was jazzy. 'Come tour my walk-in wardrobe' with Henry the VIII would actually be worth watching.[6]

Whereas now, it's not about the house, it's about the accessories and all the big wide spaces where the actual house should be, spaces that have to get filled with pointless things. Closets are the pinnacle of this. We spoke in Chapter 1, on food, about how influencers can cosplay as adults by making elaborate tea and coffee. That by involving caffeine, we will believe they have done something tiring, and I think the gigantic closet fulfils a similar function. These spaces are always reserved for something practical. It's a bedding closet. It's a 'storage space' for my Tupperware collection. It's a room for mops. This is to give the impression that the person involved puts *a lot* of work into making their beige house look nice, when in reality *a lot* of people on low wages do it for them. The (usually) women cleaning the houses would, of course, prefer there to just be *some* bedding, rather than a whole wing dedicated to it, because they also have to clean the bedding wing as there's a videographer coming over tomorrow.

Which is a great gig, BTW. Whoever worked out that owning a camera and going to massive houses to film the massive spaces really found a good niche. Like the interior designers of these houses, there isn't much expertise required – you just need to rock up and ask a few key questions.

- What's the biggest room that doesn't need to be big?
- What's the thing that your interior designer told you no

---

6 Chicken legs and dead people falling out from behind the Tudor Birkins.

one else has?

OK, let's film, starting with the:

- back-up kitchen
- child's life-size playhouse.

It is true that the child's life-size playhouse is probably the most unnecessarily big room *and* the thing that no one else has but, in the name of variety, we should just let the back-up kitchen be the opener. It is 400 square metres, after all. We know that big kitchens aren't really getting the clicks, but we can use it to pad out the video before we show everyone the child's playhouse.

The idea of a full-sized house, for a child to play in, may sound like a joke. You might think this is just another wild figment of my imagination or a concept designed to generate maximum outrage during a cost of housing crisis. I wish that were true. Unfortunately, the full-size child's playhouse does exist, and it is essentially a toy that just coincidentally manages to generate maximum outrage. It has miniature versions of everything that exists in the main house, but because the main house is literally gigantic, everything in the child's house is normal size. It's just a house for a child to run around in until they get old enough to go on TV and start telling poor people to work harder. At this point they can take their inheritance and buy another house, which I hope will not also be an exact copy of their parents' house but, given what we know about expensive houses, I'm not holding my breath.

The perfect circular economy would be for the (former) child to buy another house that has been glorified in an online video. These videos can now fulfil the functions of high-end estate agents, without having actual estate agents involved, which, I guess, is a plus. Because we live in a time where the super-wealthy actually have more in common with their global super-peers than ever before, this is really handy for showcasing housing opportunities to people who have never otherwise been to the place where your house is, but have enough money to buy it anyway. It's a bit like playing Monopoly when you live in Blackburn and saying things like, 'Urgh, I hate Old Kent Road',[7] but instead you live in Riyadh and want to buy a house in Ohio because they have recreated the Batcave from *Batman* and offer a free Robin suit for your indentured servant into the bargain.

The estate agents of TikTok are actually a whole separate category, as they are not needed in the super high-end thirst purchase industry. Those Batcaves sell themselves. The TikTok house flippers (which would have sounded like a group of very bad DJs until the world lost its mind and normalised this stuff) are similar to the investment bros, the make-up tutorial salespeople and the kid playing in their pretend house, because they pretend to do something adult and professional but, actually, just make TikToks. They then tell you that you can be rich if you think just like them and get a small starter investment from your parents. These leeches/business people buy and do up houses to be let out to people who can't get starter investments from their parents, and then they also make money by telling people that they have made money. It really is a fantastic business model. You get money, you make money from it and you make money from telling people that you make money from it. All that you need is the first bit of free money. Simple.

---

[7] I did – live in Blackburn – but I didn't know where or what Old Kent Road was. I assumed, a road.

And it is actually simple. Unlike the economics I pretended to understand earlier in the chapter, I feel like the connections between inheritance, housing and inequality are actually very intuitive. House prices in the UK grew so absurdly and so disparately for different areas between the years of 1990 and 2020 that people who bought a house at the start of this period can buy about four houses somewhere else now with just the profits they made during that time. These four houses can go to their two children. Two to live in, two to rent out. This is how there are 22-year-olds flipping houses on TikTok, because of the free money their parents got for flippin' houses.

The main reason those houses grew in value so much? Supply and demand (I am actually starting to believe that I am an economist). When there is too much of something, it gets cheaper; when there is too little, it becomes more expensive. So what happens if a population grows massively but you don't build new houses? The houses that are there become more expensive. This is economics and it is the stuff that countless people on the political right say they believe in. Yet they ignore it. They act like the surging house prices of the past 30 years are some sort of magical surprise, a result of the free hand of the market working in mysterious ways and everyone wanting to live in the UK, when, really, it's because there aren't enough of them. Because the government didn't build them. It's almost as though they already had houses that went up in value because of it and one in five of them is a landlord. Oh, wait. One in five Conservative MPs are (Booth, 2023). And they sold off the council houses and hardly built any more because poor people can live in biscuit tins or the pets'/children's houses that are left over when the owners have had enough of them.

Sorry, I seem to have been overcome by left-wingitis, but

it's hard not to be when you think that something as important as housing has been so willingly messed up by people who have been in power for so long and who are just fine themselves; people who then talk about a 'housing crisis' as if it just came out of nowhere.[8] In fact, the people who run our country often have multiple houses and, if I recall correctly, some of them used a load of public money to do the decoration (that's you, Johnson). I am sad to say that Boris didn't opt for the beige carpet, giant fish tank and Gucci sofa set. He is old money and that is why he will never make it on Insta, no matter how hard he tries.

Sorry, I seem to have been overcome by Left-wingitis, but it's hard not to be when you think that something as important as housing has been so willingly messed up by people who have been in power for so long and who are just fine themselves.

In my opinion (and I'm assuming, it's many of yours too), the idea of a Gucci sofa set should be a joke but, actually, fashion and homewares seem to have started their weird crossover period. It is not a good thing. It may be the case that Hermès and Versace have been doing wallpaper for 300 years, but I wasn't made to look at their garish nonsense in 1798, so I'm going to approach it like it's all brand new, even if it's not new for the brands. According to yours truly,

---

[8] There weren't enough houses before; there are definitely not enough now.

the stuff they are pumping out is as bad as the clothes, but possibly even sadder because sofas are life. I can let you make a horrible bag, but why are you coming for the sofas? The essential look that many of these brands go for in their homewares is 'Versailles/sweatshop'. They take the *idea* of luxury from Louis XIV and then deliver it through the medium of a factory far, far away. This is good if you want to inspire the peasants to start guillotining, while also locating your means of production at a safe distance.

Once again, the brands have outsmarted the super-rich, but they have no hope when it comes to wiley povvos. While it is a depressing reality that povvo smarts will not get you a house (sorry to all those who thought it was buying avocado toast and takeaway coffees that was stopping us), being shrewd can make the house you live in far nicer than the monstrosities on the Internet. You may live somewhere small, you may have family members in the next room and your pets may not have their own miniature home within your home but, remember, the alternative is living in a giant, beige ghost mansion. Being close to family can be a good thing, and cats do not need lifts. They like to jump. So let's stop talking about *houses* and start talking about *homes* (imagine I interlock my fingers together when I say that and do a weak, watery smile).

Big houses may be where the likes are, but home is where the... OK, you get it. We all want to live in nice, normal houses but, for now, we may live at our family home or in a shared flat, which quite often are the opposite of nice or normal. They are experiences, though.

Take living at home longer than you would have liked to. You are in your late twenties and you think the normal thing is to have moved out by now, as you spend a lot of time looking at people on the Internet who live in cavernous mansions. Your mum bangs on the ceiling of the kitchen (your room) to wake you up at 11 because, *SOCIAL MEDIA IS NOT A JOB. YOU NEED TO GET UP AND GET A JOB.*[9] She loves you.

Now think about the alternative. You could live in the cavernous mansion. Your live-in PA[10] could send a buzz over your intercom at 5 a.m. to tell you to get up and put loads of make-up on so you can make a reel about how you 'Just Woke Up Like This'. Social media is your job. Your PA hates you. Do you feel a swelling sense of gratitude now accompanying the banging of the broom on your bedroom floor? Do you see that love represented through the medium of a sweeping brush is better than a cold, professional distance pervading your *own home*. Do you think social media is a job? (If yes, contact my mum at...)

Or you may be renting. Your housemate sheds body hair like a grizzly in the shower and labels their food (*You can't be dirty* and *neurotic, Kevin, it's one or the other*). There is another guy that you have seen maybe once. You think he may be a gamer/streamer, but he is undoubtedly a stinker. You would like to move out, but in the two years since you arrived, the average cost of a room in your area has gone up by about £200 a month (insert relevant currency here). When you factor in that you would like to live in a nicer, less hairy, less smelly place, you can only assume that you would be paying at least £400 more. That is not an option. First, be kind to yourself. This is an annoying situation. Feel some pity for a bit aaaaand now do something about it. Tell Kevin you will respect his food labels if he respects your hairy shower

---

9 Honestly don't know where that came from...
10 Sort of like an au pair for rich adults.

principles. Buy some incense (from a corner shop or someone from a culture where incense is not a money-grabbing exercise, as – rule of thumb – if you are incensed by the price of incense, use sense). Now if this doesn't sort it out, then set up property alerts for about one thousand different flats that are within your price range. It's not ideal, but one will be better. I know this sounds a bit Molly-Mae therestwentyfourhoursintheday (Hague, 2022) but, really, the alternative here is just accepting a hairy, smelly life, and if you can't do that, then you have to do something else. So use your free time to look at those other shared flats. Get out. If you can't, then get comfortable, try to make your room an oasis of calm and use some of these tips.

Free things. A benefit of living in a consumerist world is that there are a lot of people out there with things they no longer want or need. Websites like Freecycle have heaps of free and fun homeware that is yours if you take the time to find it. Even if there isn't something you like, you can combine the free things to make something you do. An ugly but nicely shaped chair? A pretty throw that seems useless? Now you have a pretty throw-covered chair. I'm living my best daytime TV home makeovers life right now and there is no stopping me from changing rooms. Also remember our old friends, **samples?** They work in this space too. There are sample paints and sample wallpapers, and if you stick them on to something you got for free, things start looking artisan pretty quickly.

A lot of povvos recommended thrifty ways to create interesting spaces. Fairy lights are relatively cheap. Interesting pictures from old magazines are free. You can buy stickers that look like marble or distressed wood. If we are willing to put some serious **arts and crafts spirit** into making a room beautiful, there is no stopping us. I just did up my room along those lines and, honestly, I think it's better than most on the Internet. It's personal, I feel connected to it and I know that I can update it for almost nothing when I decide to. It doesn't matter if you get it slightly wrong, it's shabby chic. It doesn't matter that you've got a Peppa Pig night light, spray paint it gold. Now you look rich and... er... not five. Frame some book covers on the wall and call it art. You are an interior designer now.

The alternative is to **choose minimalism.** This is a powerful povvo hack as it uses the logic of the bougie to generate opportunities for those without cash. Minimalism is somehow considered the classy look. The expensive one. When it is, literally, minimal. This is a great con that has been pulled on the upper classes, but there is no reason for us not to take advantage of their error. You can choose to have a white room, with a mattress on the floor (futon), no storage for your no stuff and an **Aldi candle turned backwards,** to make it look like a Jo Malone. If you keep the space clean, it will look as though you've paid Marie Kondo £10,000 to sort your life out, but you'll be able to keep that non-existent £10,000 and all the cash you *would* have spent on things like tables, drawers and a bed. You will also, necessarily, be pure of heart and spirit, and your candle can spark joy in your uncluttered mind.

If you SIMPLY MUST have THINGS, which is a the alternative to true minimalism, go second-hand, but remember to base yourself in rich people areas when you do. The same applies online. Set your location to somewhere that is very much not your location and you can (appear to) move up in the world. Or better still, go to the **tip.** No, I am not joking. Tips or dumps often put aside some of the better things that are brought in and sell them on the cheap. Again, you have to work on cultivating some joy in being a tip-scuttler, just like you have to see the fun in designing your own interiors, but when you do, you get fun items and a free, fun experience. Think of it like the Burberry video game where, instead of LIMITED EDITION NFTs, you collect limited edition forgotten goods. They are limited because they are located in a tip on the outskirts of your town, but if you can get to know the staff there, then you can get an unlimited supply of these editions. You can also pretend that the man who works at the tip is a sort of non-player character in the Dump-Diver (we're gonna work on the name) Game, who can direct you towards prizes in exchange for kind words. This saves you buying a console. So swap numbers and they will call when expensive-looking things arrive for you. It's like having a personal shopper who is saving you money rather than spending it on the fifth floor of Harrods.

I'm aware that I need to practise what I preach and, in this instance, I might need to practise my **DIY skills** because I do not have any. It is clear to me that I should. With a small amount of effort and the help of a kindly (probably older) adviser, learning DIY skills opens up a world of cheap homewares. How hard can it be to varnish something? Well, maybe a *bit* hard, but not beyond us – we're resourceful and we are going to have some spare time, now that we're no longer looking at rich people's houses on the Internet. If we can learn the basics of sewing, sanding, varnishing and painting, we will surely be well on the way to having unlimited, personal homewares.

Or you could just **roll up your towels.** Performative bedding and towel storage is not only for influencers, it can be for you too. So take your Primark towels and roll them up like you live your life in beige. Wrap some string around them – it's rustic chic. Just because we don't have expensive things doesn't mean that we can't store them as though they are, and if I've learnt one thing from being on the Internet far too much these past few years, storing things well is the hallmark of a classy life.[11]

Like all good things, creating the perfect home gets easier if we practise (I assume), and, given all the time we are saving on

> **How hard can it be to varnish something? Well, maybe a bit hard, but not beyond us – we're resourceful and we are going to have some spare time, now that we're no longer looking at rich people's houses on the Internet.**

buying things, we have some spare to get that practising in. So, practise until your home is perfect, and until you have perfected the skills that will help you make it into whatever you want. Your home is whatever makes you happy, no matter what the social media beigeocracy tells us. Then, someday, when you die, the National Trust will buy your one-bed in Burnley and sell day tickets to people who want to take pictures of your Aldi candle, floor bed and feature wall. Then you can rock up to the lords and ladies of yesteryear in the afterlife canteen and show them how many more likes you've got than them on the National Trust's Insta.

Then, truly, the povvos will have inherited the earth, the heavens and the homes. We just have to learn to rely on the people at the dump rather than Tory politicians.

----

[11] Spoiler alert: it's not.

BEG YOUR PAR[
ROUND BALLY IO
RICH, YOU'RE PO
SPOKEN LIKE A
POVVO, BECAUS
IOT AN ANIMAL
VHY?, BECAUSE
OU'RE A POVVO
VHAT ON GOD'S
EARTH, ON TODA
EPISODE OF..., R(
SISTER SHERRIE
IAVE A DAY OFF
GASP, STOP IT I

TRAVEL
MY PERSONALITY IS DUBAI

Travel may broaden the mind, but it doesn't half narrow the pocket. It's a sad truth, and even sadder when your mind is already broad enough, some would say *too broad*, and you just want to go on holiday. Your only solution in this situation is to re-narrow your mind somewhat by watching people go on holiday on social media. This has the added benefit of also narrowing your eyes into little squinty crow's feet as you sneer at yet another person who had the world at their fingertips and decided to go to Dubai. Yes, you have to accept that this means you only have Dubai at your fingertips, but you can scroll on to someone somewhere better if you would prefer not to make those crow's feet a permanent fixture.

Or maybe you just like the crow's feet. You see, we have yet to talk about whether we all actually enjoy being annoyed at people on social media. I think we may. I call it the *Apprentice* effect. Most people don't watch *The Apprentice* to see people being good at business, making the right decisions and generally doing the reasonable things that would make anyone a good employee to a cantankerous merchant with a cockney accent. If you're like me, you watch *The Apprentice* to see people do it badly. Like me, you want to see people who claim that they are, *statistically speaking*, the smartest person in *most* British rooms,[1] present CVs that are just filled with clip art pictures of boats[2] and then create an imaginary airline that they brand exclusively with images of explosions.[3] Then watch them blame it on Sharon who wasn't even in their team.

Just as many of us don't watch *The Apprentice* to appreciate good business people, maybe we don't watch

---

[1] Real *Apprentice* line (Rein, 2017).
[2] Real *Apprentice* CV (Weather Maker, 2015).
[3] You guessed it. Real (*The Apprentice* UK, 2021).

influencers go to Dubai because we want to see good holidays. This now strikes me as so blindingly obvious that I'll have to develop the theory to even make it worth saying. I think we partly tune in for the warm, snide joy of watching people go on really bad *expensive* holidays, but mostly just enjoy doing the mental arithmetic for how many average holidays we could churn out for the price of one influencer trip. It can't be about their holidays, it can only be about ours, and you couldn't pay me to go on a holiday to Dubai. I think we are all also interested in *how* they try to make these trips look like fun. The mechanics of it. The *effort*. It's imagining the internal mental turmoil of someone on their sixth dune buggy of the day or fifth skyscraper, attempting to look happy. In the same way that an *Apprentice* candidate may not be interesting, and clip art of boats may not be either, but watching the cogs whirr as they try to make it seem clever certainly is. Dubai holidays are entertainment in the way that 'Try Not to Laugh' videos are, except many of these people are just 'trying not to look bored'.

Dubai holidays are entertainment in the way that 'Try Not to Laugh' videos are, except many of these people are just 'trying not to look bored'.

Which is a shame as the content in Dubai could be much more interesting if people weren't basically being paid to advertise Dubai by being there (Walton, 2020). This is because, to me, Dubai is like a parody of the modern world and that *is* interesting. A super-city in a desert fuelled by fossil-fuel wealth and amplified by social media nonsense is *intriguing*. It brings together everything that is wrong with our climate, economies and aesthetics in one handy package and proves that, with enough money, you can make more money without a care for anywhere outside its bubble. This could make for a great documentary or a long thought piece by an influencer, but I doubt that either of these things will happen because their aim is not to inform me about Dubai but to make me want to go on holiday there. I do not want to go on holiday to Dubai, for all the above reasons. But many people do and, in the influencers' case, they act like they do because they are being paid to. This is an important reminder that *you cannot be paid to go on holiday*. It is wild that I even feel I have to say that as, I am sure you are all aware, work is the thing you get paid for and holidays are the other way round, but this distinction seems to have been lost. So this chapter is really about people whose job it is to pretend to go on holiday, and about the rest of us who maybe pretend to work so that we can pay to go on holiday.

The prime example of this is travel blogging. Travel blogging is a career, just one where the bloggers aren't allowed to admit, like journalists used to, that they are going for work. There are none of the caveats that you need in a newspaper piece about mini-breaks, costs aren't really explained and we are supposed to believe that we are watching someone whose life just involves wandering around. This person should pretty much enjoy everything. It's a genius move because, whereas critics or journalists have to give informed views on subjects that sometimes end up negative, bloggers can pretend to like almost everything and therefore get paid for anything. Anyone who has been on holiday knows that you actually don't enjoy a number of things, but the travelblogstaverse tricks us into thinking that these people we are watching are just so much better at travelling, nay, life, than us, so they find joy in every moment, when, actually, they've been paid to enjoy it. We could all pretend to enjoy food poisoning and queuing at waterparks for the camera if we were getting paid for it.

Travel blogging is mostly based on a clever ruse that allows people to get paid and give almost no useful information. This is not always the case. There are some people out there who do short, informative videos on places for which my only other source of information is poorly translated Google reviews. These people are useful, and they save you from eventually spending 30 minutes looking at the profile of one particularly rude commenter to see if they are always this grouchy or if the place in question was *really* that bad. I'll save you the trouble and confirm that he is generally grouchy.

So, put aside any fears you may have that I am going for your favourite *useful* blogger. They get a pass. This is true of any of the Internet industries I'm talking about in this book. There are people who do communicate well, inform and educate others on the Internet and social media. But there are also people who, instead of providing information, offer sensations and feelings, which are more about escapism and envy than education or information. Nowhere is this more often the case than in the van life community. First things first, how nuts is it that I can say the words 'van life community' and you not only know what I mean but can also picture people who have an apparently aspirational life. The fact that living in a van is presented as a *better alternative* to something is, in my eyes, an indictment of what life has become like outside vans. Vans may have got marginally better (they've added kitchens and beds), but it can only mostly be that everything else has got worse.

Vans, or nomadic lifestyles in general, have mostly come up second best to static life (we're the static life community here) because of the fundamental problem that, unless you are a forager or tracking wild bison, it is harder to support yourself or contribute to a community while moving, and this means that communities are unlikely to give you the things you need for survival in return. Most jobs are hard to retain if you live in a van, which is ironic because having a van is one of the few types of ownership that is also a job in its own right. Man and van. You've seen the flyers. Just having the thing means you are employable. This would not work for, say, owning a beanbag, 'I AM *man and beanbag*, HIRE ME' doesn't work. Man and tortoise doesn't generate employment opportunities. Unless you get loads of them and do parties, which I doubt the tortoises would like.

So, having a van either = a job or less chance of a job. It's confusing maths, but we understand it intuitively. This was all clear and fine until people worked out that having a van *and a camera* DOES constitute a job. This peeves me, mainly because it messes with my view of the possibility of a van–pet–job trifecta. I think that you can only really have two of the three, you can't achieve a trifecta. You can have a job and a pet, but you don't get to gallivant around in a van. Equally, you can live in a van with a dog, but that is pretty much the definition of being someone without a job. And, well, if you have a job and live in a van, someone would always step in if you tried to get a pet. 'It's too much, Darren, you can't have it *all*.' Now, people *do* get to have it all because they have a *camera*. The camera converts inanimate objects into jobs, as it has done for make-up, houses and 'love'. Which is magical and wrong.

So, yeah, people get to live in a van *and* have a job. Which is unfair but, in return, it appears to me like they have to spend their whole life only talking about living in a van. The discomfort of this is best expressed through the medium of a 'Would you rather… ?', which would go something like this.

'Would you take complete freedom, the ability to live wherever you want and the money to live in any location you choose, in exchange for all your personality?'

'My *what*?'

'All your personality. You will essentially cease to exist apart from being a mouthpiece for vans.'

'Why? How?'

'Just think of the van like a parasite that initially starts by coexisting *with* you, the host species, before it eventually consumes you and subsumes your personality into its greater plan, which is to convince everyone else to live in vans and therefore spread the parasite. And you have to poo in the woods.'

If, in answer to this conundrum, you said, 'I'll live in the hairy shower flat from Chapter 5 over this', congratulations, you haven't been contaminated. If you chose 'freedom', then you should see a specialist and tell them how recently you have been in contact with a Mercedes Sprinter or Ford Transit.

Maybe you are just a true free spirit, though. Maybe you *already* like talking about vans but the local handymen have grown tired of you muscling in on their chats. Maybe you are quite young, attractive and have £50,000 to spare. If these things are the case, then I give you my blessing to go and become a van-life influencer. You do not have to actually be a free spirit or enjoy talking about vans *yet*, but you will need to be quite attractive and have £50,000, as van-lifers are all quite attractive and vans cost about £50,000 (new, for the van, but you will need more for the modifications). You will also need a camera and the ability to type the words, 'Five things I wish I knew...' or 'Five things you need to know...'. If you have this level of written English, are quite attractive and have a minimum of £50,000 spare, please come in. Your parasite will see you now.

I'm not kidding about the attractiveness and £50,000 – they are both essential. People have been living on the road for a long time, but rarely attractive or rich people. We weren't tuning into someone's uncle who was having a hard time after a bad divorce and living in his work van. He was not telling us 'Five things I wish I'd known before...' marrying his ex-wife. OK, maybe he *was* telling us that, but he wasn't outlining the best woods to poo in or explaining how to keep the spark alive when you are each other's wood-to-poo-in-spotter. The people have to look nice and the van has to look nice. You also have to frame it as a choice, and a good one.

That is until, of course, van-lifers discovered a whole separate and, arguably, more fruitful content line, which was *complaining* about van life. This was a clever move: it 2Xd their output almost immediately and allowed them to have one set of fans who wanted to live in vans and a whole other set who were smug because they didn't. The complaining about living in vans has become a very lucrative approach and, from what I can see, it now makes up more than half the content. You might think that this would open up the space to the hard-done-by uncle but, unfortunately, although he loves complaining about living in a van, he just doesn't have the look or the positive spins. You need to look nice and successfully balance the negative and positive, complain and *explain*. 'Van life is actually so hard on the body... That's why I do yoga' works, whereas 'Van life is actually so hard and surprisingly expensive, particularly because my ex-wife has remarried but still expects child support' doesn't. 'It's hard to find privacy when you live in a van, that's why I love the mountains' works, but 'I don't like living in a van – it's dirty, but my boss says I can't "shower" in the car park because I'm scaring the customers' doesn't.

Another common complaint is that van life is lonely (but I do lots of reading/love getting to know myself) and this is an effective content stream for lone vanners, even though they should probably have seen it coming. 'I live alone, not only alone but out of society, and it makes me feel alone' is not a shocking statement. If a vanner is so unfortunate as to have *other people* with them, because they are a couple or a family, then they have to find alternative ways to talk about vans. While these hardworking vantasists do not get to make videos about being lonely, they do get to make videos about being in love, in a van. This is a lot like being in love not in a van, except there is a van.

There are also numerous beautiful sunsets, and the option to present your picturesque love in the locations of your choice. While most lovestagrammers have to get on a plane to find a backdrop for their love, van couples can just drive there and find somewhere 'unique'. This allows them to appeal to people who don't believe in Dubai as a holiday destination or think Paris as a first date location is weird (THEY MEAN YOU, THEY'RE TRYING TO CLAIM YOU).[4] It is clever, as the main problem with love on Instagram is that it appears incredibly convoluted and fake but, somehow, by presenting the love through the medium of vans, otherwise shrewd viewers

----

[4] If you found yourself wanting to defend van people, but not Dubai people, ask yourself why? Cos they've got you.

believe the people must be genuine. 'They live in a van, surely they can't just be showing off for Instagram?'

In fact, they are, but credit to lovers in vans, they do show off in far more subtle and far less off-putting ways than their counterparts not in vans. Showing off about being in love beside a sunset is cringe, but far less so than showing off about being in love in first class on a plane. This is because planes are used across social media as status markers. They can be shorthand for 'I'm very rich' (private), 'I'm quite rich' (first class), 'I'm being paid to go' (business class) and 'I'm actually a real person' (just a plane, probably Wizz[5] Air). It is surprising that social media took so long to catch on to the potential of planes for generating class-based frustration because airlines realised it a very long time ago. Why do you think they put first class at the front and make us all walk through it? Why do we gradually have to descend from somewhere very nice and peaceful, to somewhere slightly less nice, until we find ourselves in the back seat that can't recline beside the toilet? Because you need to SEE what you could have won if you were rich or paid to pretend to be. You and the five crying, unaccompanied babies that inexplicably are the other passengers in your row (how did they book the seats?), you all need to know that you must do better. Sadly, you are too old to get rich now, but the babies still might make it. If they just grow up, stop crying and start collecting some clip art boats for their CVs.

Airlines have known for a long time that jealousy is a powerful motivator but social media realised far later. Now we are all stuck looking at first-class flights when we are not

---

[5] Maybe so named because they are going to start charging to take a wizz?

on planes and feeling short-changed when we are. Even when we are doing something so great as going on holiday, and doing something as amazing as FLYING IN THE SKY. The frustration of flying, and the jealousy injected into it by the mix of lounges, speedy boarding and baggage weights ('Yes, I will put on all the clothes I would have packed to get my bag below the weight limit. I know it looks odd, but do you have a policy on how many clothes I can wear? No? Well, then, it's my right') blinds us all to the fact that we are getting to do something that 99.9 per cent of humans in the whole of history would agree was equivalent to having godlike powers. We fly in the sky. To a completely different place in the world. And it's *so annnnnnoying*.

Which makes me sound like I am super-zen and don't find it annoying myself. I do. I don't achieve the standards I set for myself. I have accepted that and I hope you can too. I hope you can also accept that I do go on holiday, sometimes. I know that people just want me to stay in my bed and generally be a bitter man in a onesie, but I need to get out there occasionally.

The truth is, povvos have been going on holidays for a long time. There was the Canterbury Tales Pilgrim Povvo Package Holiday back in the Middle Ages and the Victorian povvo penchant for a trip to Blackpool or Brighton. We have a right to holiday, and we will be damned if we don't take one and make it cheap. And my, do we make it cheap, judging by the tips I got. I was overwhelmed by the frugal beauty of it, so I'm going to try to get as

We have a right to holiday, and we will be damned if we don't take one and make it cheap.

much in as possible by outlining a WHOLE holiday, because there is a lot of useful stuff in there for navigating the potential costs. There is a challenge to being cheap on a holiday, but we rise to it. You may be away from the safety of home, the freezer and the safety nets that you have built up to keep things cheap, but if you pack your smarts, you will be fine – flourish, even. So let's get into it.

The first question for a holiday is 'Where?' The answer, of course, is anywhere BUT HERE, but a cheap option is 'somewhere close to home'. In which case, remember, **a holiday in your own country is not a staycation, it is a holiday.** Don't let them tell you your domestic trip is less in any way than a trip abroad, and keep believing that your caravan in the rain is just as much a holiday as a selfie-based excursion to a fabricated beach in Dubai. Such a trip can be even cheaper if you **only go somewhere where you know people, for free accommodation.** This has the added benefit of making it seem like *you* have made the effort to see someone when, really, you are just looking for a free bed. You get gratitude *and* a roof over your head. Win. This approach is also often combined with the **travel with extended family** option, to achieve economies of scale and the wisdom of aunties (the economy of scales/price per kg). You will have to accept, of course, that this means you will spend time with your family.

Which is a challenge, but at least one of them will probably **pack their own tea/coffee/lunch.** My family can't go to Blackpool without bringing along, essentially, an entire takeaway menu of food, so I'm glad to see that many of you feel it is a good thing too. This was the first of the packing-based tips I received, which is second only to rinsing hotels in the hierarchy of holi-pov advice.

Next, you must remember that *how* you pack will set the tone for everything else you do. A cheap holiday starts when you pack your bag, so remember that **hand luggage travel is always possible.** Do not get suckered into the checked baggage. If you just believe hard enough, you *can* become Mary Poppins, but you should also remember to roll and squeeze every item of clothing you are going to take, only pack one pair of shoes and, if you *must* have a second pair, squeeze socks and pants into them to save space.

Sticking to hand luggage is the first victory you can win over the airlines, but you know it doesn't stop there. They want you to buy duty-free, but make *them pay you* by **maxing out on perfume testers until you smell disgusting.** 'What are you wearing? You smell strong... and... varied?' 'Yes, it's Paco Rabanne–CK–MUGLER–DKNY– CK one–temptation–Summer Breeze–Flowerbomb. Nice, isn't it?'

It's not, but it's the smell of success. You smell bad but feel good. Now go to the gate, do not get distracted by the array of chain restaurants and shops. Sit there. Wait. **DO NOT SPEEDY BOARD.** Watch the speedy boarders get into the queue they've paid to queue in marginally earlier than you and feel proud – you are basically being paid to queue slowly. So take your slow queue on to the tarmac and up those rickety steps, and hold your head high as you pass the people with extra legroom and seats at the front. You have **filled an empty bottle with water from a fountain** after the security checks and now you can settle down to a nice meal of **squashed sandwiches for the flight.** You know the squashing only makes them better, and you'd rather eat any of them than one of those airline paninis. Your holiday has begun.

Now if you're lucky enough to be going abroad, and *wild* enough to be staying in a hotel (A HOTEL), then there are ways to make it work. Some advice is obvious. **Steal the soap.** It's not stealing in the way taking loo rolls from restaurants is, because the hotel *expects* it. That's why they put their branding and name all over each tiny bottle, because you are effectively providing free marketing every time you take them out later on your trip. So fear not. You may also decide to take the batteries from the TV remote and the bulbs from the lamps, but that is bordering on toilet roll theft territory.

If the hotel has breakfast, remember to **go hard on the buffet, so you won't need lunch.** Yes, you will effectively be in a food coma between the hours of 10 and 2 and you'll have to take regular breaks to stop and burp in the shade somewhere, but that's passive income right there. If you are really smart, you will do as my mother does and pack a few of the leftovers. By 'leftovers', I mean cold cuts, bread rolls, cheese, a little yogurt pot and maybe some beans in a plastic tub she brought down with her. This will allow you to **make a packed lunch with the things from breakfast.** You probably won't need lunch as you wheeze around some landmark that you are too full to appreciate, but keep those sweating goods safe because you never know when the temptation to actually pay for a meal will strike you. If the urge doesn't arrive during the day, don't worry, you can just store your supplies in the hotel mini-fridge, which would otherwise only hold £5 Diet Cokes (DO NOT TOUCH THEM).

After you have fallen asleep in a dark museum, you will feel re-energised and this is a great time to **follow a tour group around.** You can learn about the wonders of the local culture (in German) and develop an interest in the culture of the tour group you have joined (two for the price of one). Yes, you may have to pretend you are Japanese or Portuguese for an hour or two and, yes, you may not understand anything you are taught, but you get to be part of something for once. That little flag the person at the front is waving, that is for you, and if the flag-waving overlord does notice you, just pretend to, coincidentally, be walking the same route as them. It's a free country, *senpai*, I'm just looking at this wall.

When they have finally kicked you out, or the woman at the back has become so scared of you that you simply must go, find time for an ice cream. I've made my feelings on ice cream clear in Chapter 3, but I have not shared that the only thing better than an ice cream is a *holiday* ice cream. The only thing better still is one from a **Lidl multipack.** I cannot stress enough how much you need to **find the Lidls in advance.** They are everywhere, and if they are not (because you are somewhere suuuuuper-exotic), find their equivalent – maybe an Aldi. A six-pack of ice cream sandwiches from a supermarket is gonna set you back around the same amount as one single ice cream in town, so know where to find them. Yes, they may be a long walk from the beach, but you need to burn off some of that breakfast (the fourth trip up to the buffet was too much, we know that now). When you get back to the beach, you will thank yourself, and you can get down to the serious business of... er, being on the beach. Now, this one doesn't really apply to me but for those of you who value it, this next tip is for you: **rich people can afford a tan, you have one week, so value the burn.** I don't think I can endorse this, because of the whole skin cancer issue, but if you want a tan, just buy some really bad suncream, you know the kind that is basically murky water, so at least you are pretending to do the right thing by your skin (you're not).

If you do have a home to go back to (a holiday home), most likely because you have travelled with family and therefore have crammed 11 people into a two-bedroom Airbnb, remember to **cook dinner** mostly. This is a beautiful communal event, where you can get to know local foods and come to understand the incredibly insular eating habits of your extended family. The phrase 'foreign' may be used by an older relative and that is an experience we all need to have. Should you feel fancy enough to go out for a meal, **skip the drinks and dessert** but, remember, there are plenty of supermarket-bought beverages at home and multipacks on multipacks of Maxibons in the freezer.

You will feel richer for having holidayed, and certainly be richer for having holidayed like a true povvo. I hope the advice has helped, although I do get the sense that you probably live by most of these principles already. The holiday commandments are somehow passed down in povvo genetic memory, as if we've been doing it since the pilgrimage days. This might be the reason that I am so offended by the modern trend for holidays, for the commercialised Dubai trip and the perennial holidays of the van-lifers. Holidays are meant to be short, cheap and challenging, not tours of expensive places you saw on social media. I know it deep in my bones and I am proud because, while the holidays of online influencers may have a

You will feel richer for having holidayed, and certainly be richer for having holidayed like a true povvo.

lot in common with the bad candidates of *The Apprentice*, our holidays are more like the winners. We find deals, get things done quickly and boats never appear in our itineraries or on our CVs.

We may still take credit for things we have not done, rush wildly around a foreign city looking for absurd items and blame our holiday teammates when things go wrong, though. How hard is it, really, to speak pretend German, Mum?

BEG YOUR PAR
ROUND BALLY I
RICH, YOU'RE PO
SPOKEN LIKE A
POVVO, BECAUS
NOT AN ANIMAL
WHY?, BECAUSE
YOU'RE A POVVO
WHAT ON GOD'S
EARTH, ON TODA
EPISODE OF..., R
SISTER SHERRII
HAVE A DAY OFF
GASP, STOP IT

WORK AND PRODUCTIVITY

WHAT IN THE MATILDA NONSENSE IS GOING ON HERE?

Social media never fails to surprise me. I think that is why I've never left. It may have left me bitter, jaded and frustrated to the point of writing a whole book about how bonkers it can be, but it's kept me on board. I think it's because I love those surprises. So here's a surprise for the day. I have decided on the single worst corner of the Internet.

It's work and productivity.

That's not even the surprise, though. No, the real shock is that I *keep* thinking I've found the worst part of how some of us use social media and keep convincing myself that my reasons for thinking it are somehow more valid than the last time I made the decision. When I wrote about food on social media, I was *sure* it was the worst, because we *need* food. Then I started thinking about Internet love and I changed my mind. No, that was worse, they're ruining *literal love*. I was certain it was game over and now, here we are, because, surprise, surprise, work and productivity culture has come along and stolen the top spot.

I really believe it this time (again). This is a special case. Work and productivity as presented by social media are *the* worst things on there. I await your suggestions for something better[1] (or should that be worse?), but it is a hard task because productivity on the Internet has one thing going for it that no others have, one aspect that will always and for ever make it more ridiculous than the others. You want to know? It's that: **contradiction 1: WATCHING SOMEONE ON THE INTERNET TALK ABOUT BEING PRODUCTIVE IS NOT PRODUCTIVE.**

Sorry, was I shouting? Shouting is not productive.

NEITHER ARE YOU, INTERNET PRODUCTIVITY CULTURE.

---

[1] Surprise me.

Sorry, I'm a bit het up. Let me start again. I'll take some deep, calming breaths, do the Pomodoro technique, journal and spend four hours a day watching someone talk about how effective their life is. Then, and only then, will I have something productive to say.

The reason this field of social media stands out from the others is that it is based on an actual, evident logical contradiction. Unless your job is watching videos on the Internet, you *cannot* be productive by watching videos on the Internet. Unlike every other way of wasting time on social media, this is the only one that sells itself as a way to stop wasting time. Doing it undoes what it is teaching you to do. It's like food videos on TikTok somehow making you unable to eat. Or fashion on Instagram immediately turning your own clothes to dust.

Unless your job is watching videos on the Internet, you cannot be productive by watching videos on the Internet.

Some of you may not know what I mean when I talk about work and productivity on the Internet, so I should clarify. You probably have a genuinely productive life where you don't watch people outline their daily routine, tell you how to digitally detox via their digital platform and explain how to become a millionaire by telling other people how to tell other people how to become a millionaire. Good for you. Well, work and productivity on social media comprise all those things. People tell you how effective they are. They post videos of themselves being effective and sometimes even tell you how they became so effective, as well as sharing the results of this effectiveness (lots of money). In reality, these videos are only effective at generating contradictions and subscription fees, but they do vary in terms of the contradictions they offer in return for your subscription. Yes, the method that someone uses to show you how to be better will determine the sort of contradictions they offer, so let's start first with one of my favourite incoherence-generators, 'daily routines'.

The 'My Daily Routine' video has been a staple of social media for a few years now, so if it's new to you, then you've done so well. The basic format is that someone pretends to show you a normal day in their life, which is usually inexplicably perfect and, inexplicably, has a camera there the whole time. Which brings us to **contradiction 2: YOUR DAILY ROUTINE IS NOT YOUR DAILY ROUTINE IF YOU ARE FILMING IT ALL.**

You'll just have to get used to the shouting at this point. They can't hear me at the back over all the tippy-tappy productivity and the bubbling of the matcha lattes. This contradiction is oh so simple (not to be confused with Oats So Simple, which, to the best of my knowledge, has never once been involved in a daily routine video, but does actually make for quite a quick and productive breakfast). It almost needs no explanation. I call it 'The Reality TV' problem. If you are setting up a camera, checking you look beautiful in the footage and editing together a montage to the soundtrack from 'Harvest Moon', you are breaking your daily routine. The only way that your daily routine video could ACTUALLY be accurate is if you only ever made daily routine videos. Every day. You would also have to have a camera filming the bits where you were filming yourself pretending to do things like work. This has the potential to spiral into an infinite loop of cameras filming the cameras filming the cameras, which would be hard on the eyes (*not* what daily routine videos are about) and deeply ineffective. Which wouldn't actually be a problem because **contradiction 3: your effective daily routine is not effective, as you are spending a lot of time filming yourself.**

This is an issue if you are pretending to do an actual job in your daily routine videos. If you admit that your only job is filming yourself, you will be fine, but in most routine videos people like to have a segment where they highlight things and open a really nice MacBook, to signify that they do work.[2] This means that spending hours of your day filming is a problem because you couldn't do an actual job as well. Imagine you had to make a film about *your* job one day. It would have to actually be a good film that looks nice, so you couldn't just leave a camera in the corner of the office and upload the CCTV footage to Vimeo at 6:00 when you went home.

You would have to set up the tripod, while ignoring Deborah from Accounts, who really needs you to give an opinion on a budget. You would be required to do a second take of yourself pretending to type productively while not emailing a client before a deadline and you would have to edit all the footage at the end of the day, during your mid-year review. When you'd be fired because YOU HAVE BEEN MAKING A FILM ALL DAY AND NOT WORKING.

Which is OK because at least you can spend more time with your kids. Maybe you can film *their* routine? Oh, sorry, did you not hear? There are children's daily routine videos as well. Let's look past the fact that this is effectively child labour (if not less arduous than most examples of it) and home in

---

[2] Or write 'Work from home' in a nice notebook and then cross it out. If only it was always that easy.

on the fact that someone is making their child pretend to be efficient, to get themselves more Instagram likes and (I think) sell gadgets.

The likes bit I won't even dwell on. If people are following accounts to see children pretend to live strange adult-free lives, then there is no hope for them. If people want to film that Matilda nonsense, then I cannot help. I do want to dwell on what they are actually doing, which is secretly selling products. Now I know that pretending to do something and selling products in the process basically *is* social media, but I can't help but find this example a bit creepy. The way these routine videos work is that the child goes around and does lots of different things in a house using weird gadgets (a bear that prints their homework, a loo brush that comes out of a plastic egg) and the video is actually about the odd products rather than the routine.

Which, in truth, all the daily routine videos are. There is no actual work in the routines, but there are always lots of nice gadgets. A person will have a Mac, an iPad, 64 highlighters and not actually do anything with any of them. I guess this is for the best as *actually* watching a video of someone working hard would be even more boring than just seeing some nice highlighters. The hard work would be, well, hard work. I'm not saying I couldn't enjoy watching a genuine daily routine from someone who was hardworking, but it would have to be suitably chaotic, sometimes sad and, at the end, leave me respecting a person's toil. It would have to be a fly-on-the-wall documentary, like a company came in and said, 'We're just gonna film you. We'll wait here while you sleep and press record from the moment you wake up. Just be yourself.' We would have the shot of someone missing their alarm, being deeply confused about the camera crew in their room and realising that they are already too far behind in their schedule to take the time to kick them out, so just crack on with it. I'm convinced. We need a campaign to choose our own productivity influencers. I want to see the daily routine of a working single mother of four rather than a teenager cosplaying as someone with a job. There would be a lot to learn.

In my imagination, the mother of four accepts the camera crew as a necessary evil, before running to the kids' bedrooms and shouting 'UP!' If she is anything like the matriarchs in my line, she would bang on pots and pans while doing it. Then she would slam down a box of cereal and food bowls,[3] slide a bottle of milk down the table like she was Tom Cruise in that film where he makes cocktails and circle back round to the rooms to shout 'UP!' again. She would most likely know where the shoes were. You know, the ones that each of the children had somehow independently lost overnight. Slam! Front door would shut, car would start and she would find a quicker route to the school than the Waze app ever could.[4] Kids get thrown out of the car like paratroopers and, screech, she's off to work. Here we have a fast montage. Talk to someone, type something, have a meeting, eat a bad wrap. Then have a meeting, type something and talk to someone. Leave, but do some more talking/meeting/typing on the way to the car. Screech back to the children and hoover them into the back seat. Stop a vicious fight from breaking out while undertaking a lorry and arrive back home. Create an actual '15-Minute Bolognese' (take that, Jamie Oliver), but without a recipe guide alongside it in the video, as there is no time. It's mince and tomatoes, work it out, people.

---

3 I'm picturing this video with a lot of jump cuts, like an Edgar Wright film.
4 That Edgar Wright film would be *Baby Driver*.

Three children refuse the Bolognese, so they get just pasta and cheese, while the eldest enjoys the sauce. She does their homework. Then sends them all off to play 'Minecraft' while she cleans everything, locates tomorrow's lost shoes and packages uneaten bolognese for her lunch. She spends five minutes getting the kids to stop playing 'Minecraft' (then unplugs the computer). She debates the merits of toothbrushing with a five-year-old philosopher. Brings kids to their beds and says goodnight. Removes the child who has magically somehow ended up in her own bed. Gets into her own bed. She reads five minutes *of this book* and falls asleep, because it is quite possible this woman is you. Sweet dreams, you are my influencer of choice.

Camera crew leaves quietly...[5]

If it is not you, then I hope you now realise that 'taking the Instagram app off my phone' to be more productive (and then less productively scrolling through it on a web browser instead) is not what productivity looks like. It looks like that mum. And you are possibly me... because that Instagram app deletion thing is something I've tried. Productivity people on social media love telling you not to go on social media while you are on their social media page. It's part of the digital detoxification process, and the societal toxification process. You can also try to make your relationship with social media more productive by limiting your time on apps. No, I don't mean going on them less, I mean adding another piece of software that tells you when you've been on an app for too long. This allows you to use the apps as much as you ever did but gamify it, by wasting time to a deadline. You allow yourself

---

[5] Kind but unnecessary, because she's so tired she could sleep through a nuclear attack.

15 minutes, then try to stop *exactly* when the timer is up. Then you start again for another 15 minutes, until the whole day has passed and you have produced nothing. Did someone say life hack?

Productivity people on social media love telling you not to go on social media while you are on their social media page.

Using technology to improve your relationship with technology is a common theme of the productivitynet. I think this is mostly because technology is the only thing you can sell to people who want to get more work done, but also because the only work that this corner of the Internet recognises is computer-based. To my knowledge, there are no productivity gurus out there trying to make people more productive carpenters or teachers. There is seemingly no app that you can sell to a nurse to help them retain their focus. So it is a field full of people on computers telling other people who work on computers how to do more work on computers. They focus on this type of work because people who do it have a much harder time evaluating how well they are doing. Whereas a candlestick maker could count how many candlesticks they made or a farmer knows whether they have done the things they need to do, someone managing data sets can never really know if they have done enough and could always sort of do more. As a result, people end up working continually and never really feel like their work is complete, which leaves lots of room for gurus to prey on their uncertainty.

Even worse, these gurus play on the confusion between our *work* and our *self*. They say that they're making *you* a more productive person when, really, they're just telling you how to do more work in less time. If you feel like you are a better person because you get more work done, your self-esteem is tied to the productivity that gurus are selling you. If you feel like your lack of productivity is a reflection of your personality and your failings, then you are very suggestible. The productivity guru becomes an actual guru, who says they can help you to be a better person, which gives them a lot of influence.

It is also not how work *works*. The productivity of a business is the responsibility of the business's owners. They need to create systems to make their business work well, not direct you to a man on YouTube talking about life hacks. If you are doing the work you are required to do, then your job stops there. You are not paid to worry about how you could be more productive. In fact, worrying about being productive is only going to make you worse in your work. This is actually the basis of **contradiction 4: trying to be more productive will make you less productive.**

This is because a lot of the ways that people try to achieve productivity are actually quite harmful to our health and well-being. If you try to save time on meals by just drinking an 'all-in-one complete meal shake' and only sleep four hours a night, you will be an unhealthy, unhappy person. Unhealthy, unhappy people are not productive and, although we may *feel* more productive in the short term, there are always knock-on effects in the long run.

It also seems true that the more 'simple hacks' we introduce, the less productive we feel. Trying to introduce 'time blocking' or the Pomodoro technique to your schedule may help sometimes but, in general, it just adds another thing to your to-do list. Remembering to do some time blocking is one more part of your brain that you are not applying to attaining your goals, and it's one more thing to feel guilty about when you forget to do it. If you followed all the productivity tips that are put forward by the gurus, remembering and completing them would basically be a full-time job. You could spend a whole day when you were supposed to be working highlighting, batching, designing to-do lists, creating Eisenhower matrixes, colour-coding and journalling[6] with the aim of getting more work done and, in the process, get *no* work done. So ignore them, do your work and feel proud. You are doing just fine.

You may actually *like* colour-coding. I've noticed that a lot of the hacks people offer centre on putting things in order and colour-coding them. This just seems to be an incredibly popular thing to do on the Internet, in any form. Whether it is highlighting and ordering work schedules or putting all your juices in different containers, I would say that about 34 per cent of the Internet is dedicated to putting things in order. I think this is because the Internet makes us feel so disordered and disorientated. We can see everything, everywhere, at any time and we just want a way to feel less overwhelmed,[7] so people label things and highlight them and it makes everything *feel* more manageable when, in reality, we were getting by fine before we introduced all these other things. The problem is that we turn to videos of people putting things in order on the Internet to make us feel a little bit less disordered (by the Internet) but we only end up feeling less orderly than the people who are doing it professionally online. If you feel like a state

---

[6] All real productivity techniques.
[7] Just whelmed. We don't want to be underwhelmed, but a nice calm state of whelm will do it.

because you're working too hard, watching someone whose only job it is to put things in order will only make you feel worse in comparison.

So ignore the advice, and certainly do not give money to people for premium subscriptions to get their advice. There are productivity gurus out there who are making obscene amounts of money by doing this. You would think that they are offering something truly life-changing – some advice which is just *so* good they simply have to create a 'subscribers only' feed – but the truth is, they are not. If they really had such a thing, they would not be selling subs on YouTube. In most cases, the subscription is to a group where you learn how to become a productivity salesperson. I KID YOU NOT. Humanity built the pyramids with productivity (and slavery) thousands of years ago, and now our productivity is going into building pyramid schemes. If you know this is what you want to do with your life, go ahead, subscribe. Everyone might do it, and I'll end up being the last man standing. A lone, unproductive wolf with 8 billion productivity gurus trying to teach me how to be more productive as the world falls apart around us because no one is doing anything any longer. They are just talking about being productive.

It may simply be that online work is *never* going to feel as productive as making things in the real world and productivity gurus are trading on that. Maybe people just want to feel part of something. Maybe we want to know why we are all working so hard and never feel satisfied.

BUT FOR $9.99 THE SHABAZSCRIPTION WILL SHOW YOU HOW TO SUCCEED IN A ONESIE ONLINE.[8]

---

[8] Onesie sold separately. Only onesies purchased through legitimate Shabaz sales channels will be accepted.

Joking. All the advice you need is right here, and it came from all of you. So there you go, I've thrown in some community for free.

Because working – productively or otherwise, and having a laugh about it – has always been a staple of the povvo mindset. The idea of saying, 'I had a crap day at work. I really wasn't up to much', and then giggling about it with a friend, is something we have a duty to do. We must all be allowed to be crap sometimes. This should not be a controversial thought, but in the post-industrial world, you would think it was. We are told to be our best selves all the time and be ashamed if we are ever anything less. This is wrong – a bad day is a bad day and being bad at your job is not a problem, unless you are getting fired for it. So enjoy yourself and, if you are not enjoying yourself, don't feel ashamed that your life isn't giving you perfect fulfilment at every moment like the Internet tells you it should.

❮❮ ❯❯

We are told to be our best selves all the time and be ashamed if we are ever anything less. This is wrong – a bad day is a bad day and being bad at your job is not a problem, unless you are getting fired for it.

The povvo advice has begun. I will call that first piece of productivity advice, **be OK with being unproductive.** Revolutionary stuff, I know. The second and third pieces of advice are also pretty basic, but I think they have to be said: **do something you like and if you can't do something**

you like for money, try to make it fun and don't take it too seriously – it's just a job.

Doing something you like is actually a rare crossover case in terms of Internet productivity advice and 'povvo productivity preaching' (PPP).[9] This is because it is pretty obvious. We should all do things that we like to do as much as we can, at least until doing them stops us being able to do things we need to do. The list of needs can be understood as eating, sleeping, ensuring we have enough money to survive and caring for other people if they depend on us. Beyond these things, nothing is really a need, so focus on doing things you want to do at their expense. If you can do something you like for money, then great, but if you can't, don't try to convince yourself that the reason you are not happy doing it is because you are not doing it well enough or working hard enough. It's because you don't really like it. So try to make it fun as much as you can (work friends, sneaky naps, scrolling through the Internet) and accept it for what it is, something not very fun that you do in exchange for money to survive and do things you *do* like.[10] People get confused because we are told thinking like that makes you a bad person, an unproductive person, unmotivated, lazy. In reality, you are just normal and should focus on making work tolerable and the rest of your life great. No amount of productivity will magically make work you don't enjoy enjoyable.

When you have things you have to do, **just do them.** I know that sounds dangerously like productivity-speak again

---

9 Not to be confused with the Three Ps – parks, picnics and perambulation – of Chapter 3.
10 I'm a teacher, after all. No one is in this game for the money. It's the holidays. Jokes... Well...

(and Nike), but my reasons differ. My main reason is that procrastination is time that you could be using to do something enjoyable and the thing you are not doing is not gonna get any more enjoyable by pushing it back. So if you get it done as quickly as you can and then DON'T tell anyone you've finished it quickly (because they'll just give you something else to do), you'll have earnt all the time you would have spent procrastinating back to spend on resting. That is actually productive and if your boss asks you how the project is getting on, you can say, 'I'm just finishing it up now.'

The key difference between povvo productivity and the advice of online gurus is that povvos try to save time and money, while the gurus sort of expect you to pay them for the time you gain. They also expect you to use that time to just do more work, which as we have just discussed, is not the way we work.

Shopping lists are a classic povvuctivity device. By taking a small amount of time to think about what you want and need from your weekly shop, you can earn back that time by not faffing at the shops and stick to only buying things which are going to be useful during the week. In my past (confession alert), I've fallen for the tricks. I've bought things from the expensive aisle leading up to the checkout and panic-bought others that I didn't need. My shopping list is like having my mother in my pocket. It travels with me and says, 'Do you really need that?', 'When will you use it?' or 'I know the middle aisle of Aldi is fun, but buying these things won't make you *like* camping.'[11]

----

11 Also, you get the joy of ticking things off your list! It is the antidote to being overwhelmed in any situation, and if you put enough easy things on your to-do list, you can create momentum by completing them early.

If you *do* like camping, then go ahead and approach the middle aisle with your shopping list in hand. Camping is one of the great cheap holidays, so if you need an extra mat or new gas cylinder, check whether there is one on offer and have some fun. Just plan in advance, because planning is time well spent and results in money, well, not spent. This is the case for the next piece of advice, which is a productivity HACK (I'm calling it a hack because it makes me feel important and it's what the gurus do): **plan errands by location to save time and money.** This is another simple one, but it is really useful and a great antidote to the discombobulation that is most people's existence. If you can work out what you need to do in the day and where you need to do it, mark it out like a wartime general with their big table map. March on Paris (the school drop off) at 8:30 hours, take Berlin (the post office, because it's close) at 09:00 and then move on to Moscow (the big Aldi) before 10:00. Then settle down knowing that no bus fare has been left behind, no petrol wasted and peace has been secured.

If you want to go a step further, forget the bus fares and petrol and **walk everywhere.** I know this isn't an option for everyone, we all have different bodies and challenges, but if you do have a way to make your own way between errands, it's a really productive approach. In fact, I think this is ancient povvo wisdom. We have been walking for millennia. The best thing is that it also introduces health into the equation, which the productivity gurus like to pretend they care about. If you are walking, your heart rate is up but your expenditure is down. You are saving money *and* gaining a free workout. Can't say any better than that.

You also get to bank some health points, which you can

return to when you do unhealthy things like go out on the town. I got a great tip, which was **pool your money with friends before a night out so rounds are equal,** which I think is cool. There would need to be some negotiation after this point – someone might want to drink Champagne while you are teetotal – but if you can all make some agreements in advance, this saves on the frustration of the rounds system. Debbie and Dave, who get themselves water on their round and order Grey Goose on yours, need not be an issue. People who don't drink can negotiate a discount. I know people think this takes away from the carefree attitude of heading out with friends, but the truth is that, when you have no money, the laissez-faire approach to going out is the opposite of carefree, it's anxiety-inducing. So, by being a bit careful and giving the night out a little thought, you have a chance to go without breaking your bank and you may even be able to do it again before pay day.

I love how different these pieces of advice are from those in the online productivity sphere. Walk. Split your rounds. Make a shopping list. These are things that actually make life work for *us*, rather than the online courses about techniques recommended by 64 per cent of productivity scientists to make you 174 per cent more productive for *work*.

Full hands in, full hands out is another piece of advice that could only really come from a povvo because you have to have worked in the service industry to understand it (productivity gurus are rarely waiting on tables). In a restaurant, it's the idea that if you go out from back of house to serve a table with plates, make sure you come back from front of house with another set that are done with. If you bring something out, bring something back in. I think this is solid advice that can save time and money if you extend it to the rest of your life. First, I think it might help make a dent in the army of mugs that end up beside my computer, so it's handy for keeping a house clean, but, really, it could work at scale too. Go out to work and do the shopping on the way back. That's a trip saved. Getting the post from outside? Take out the bins as you do. It is basically the sort of advice that productivity gurus need to give, but they won't because they are afraid to talk about things like bins.

A piece of advice that online gurus do actually give is to **batch-cook.** Now they usually say this because they are looking to maximise their macros or save time to work more on their productivity website, but for the rest of us it's about time and money. If you have the time on a Sunday, cook a load of stuff. Use that (those) freezer(s) to good effect. Life can be hectic and saving yourself from cooking on a weeknight when you get in late or a hasty trip to a small shop (we know your tricks miniature supermarkets, you charge waaaaay more) can really make a difference. It can also be healthier, but that's your call. Cook what you like, what you can afford and what you can get done in the small amount of time you have. You will also feel hella productive.

Finally, **use your local library.** They are great places (if the government hasn't shut them) and we need to use them to keep them alive. They are free work spaces, treasure troves of information and warm, comfortable community assets that we should value. Instead of paying for coffees and sitting on a box that the café owner has repurposed as a stool, cos it's chic, sit in a comfy chair and do your work. If you need a break, read a book, there's loads of them. Afterwards, you can feel proud that you have not only been productive, but you have also helped to justify the continued existence of an institution that has introduced millions of children to the joys of reading. I hope you are reading this book in one because not paying for my book is, like, so on brand.

Whatever you do, make me the last person from social media whose advice you take on being productive.[12] Ask people you respect how they get things done, have some compassion for yourself and try to separate your self-worth from the work you do. You are so much more than your productivity, and the gurus are so much less in control than they pretend to be.

---

[12] And in truth, it's not even *my* advice. I am but a conduit for the povvo spirits of my page.

BEG YOUR PAR
ROUND BALLY IO
RICH, YOU'RE PO
SPOKEN LIKE A
POVVO, BECAUS
NOT AN ANIMAL
WHY?, BECAUSE
YOU'RE A POVVO
WHAT ON GOD'S
EARTH, ON TODA
EPISODE OF..., RC
SISTER SHERRIE
HAVE A DAY OFF
GASP...STOP IT I

HEALTH AND CLEANLINESS

I'M FIT, YOU'RE NOT

''ve always heard people say that health is wealth, but I never really understood what they meant. Until recently. I always thought they were saying that being healthy is as good as being rich. That investing in your health is a business with guaranteed returns. Then I saw a load of influencers get really rich off telling me how healthy they are and realised that I'd had it wrong all along. They mean that health is wealth because if you know how to sell it, you can have all the wealth you want. This was a wake-up call for me as I didn't really take care of my health before. Now I really don't, because if my health is their wealth, I'm going to double down[1] and be even less healthy. Each muffin I eat has become a stand (a sit-down, mostly) against those who profit from our fear of sickness. Of death.

Of course, you can't just make money by going on the Internet and telling people to be healthy – you do have to look healthy too. I have to give the wealthy, healthy influencers some credit on that front. They put a lot of work into looking nice, but they know it is essential. No one is buying spirulina off me, and the huge numbers that my 30-day fat-burn challenge is doing are mostly on my own scales. I am a bit confused, though, about what 'looking healthy' means. What is it to look healthy? How effective is the eye test really when diagnosing someone's internal function? I can tell if someone looks *unhealthy*, I understand mirrors, but I doubt that the medical profession is losing work to people who are just really good at making diagnoses based on photos of people in yoga pants. I think what we mean

---

[1] Not the KFC sandwich, which, rather than the traditional bread, uses two pieces of fried chicken as a bun, with cheese, bacon and sauces in between. I am vegetarian, so I can never find out how people don't burn their hands.

when we say people look healthy is that they look slim and clean.

So I have tied together the health and cleanliness chapters. Internet health is about looking clean and in control, and I think that is pretty much the same thing as the wealth of channels where people clean by moving things into clear plastic tubs and bottles. In my eyes, these bottles are the only transparency you will find in this corner of the Internet, which is almost as ironic as the fact that *seeming* clean can make you so filthy rich.

This is one of the reasons that people who talk about health are so often the same people who showcase cleanliness. These fields both trade on the desire for order and control that we discussed in Chapter 7, about work and productivity. Health and cleanliness on social media are two more responses to the disordering effects of the Internet on people. They are responses to the ways in which the modern world has made many of us unhappy and ill. They are just not very good ones. Health and cleanliness influencers cannot be the solution to the sicknesses of modern life (most of which are social and psychological) because their performances of wellness are just not convincing. They seem to be... wound up a bit tight, you could say. A man who irons his bed sheets on his bed is not someone I will turn to for advice on well-being, and a woman who writes down everything she eats is not providing a solution to the anxiety of modern existence.

I think the problem is much the same as it is for productivity – we are looking for solutions to a problem that we cannot diagnose. We don't think that we are sick, but many of us are sure we are not entirely well. We turn to obsessive people with low body fat as a substitute for functioning healthcare systems, and the solutions to a society that has been massively disrupted by the rapid advance of technology. We are dealing with a malaise that we feel but cannot explain. More people than ever say they feel tired most of the time, yet the types of work we are doing are less strenuous than ever. Medical science is the best it has ever been, yet so many of us do not feel well. In neoliberal societies, we blame ourselves. The paranoid and ultimately convincing answer for why we feel off, we are told, is that *we* are simply not being healthy enough. Society isn't making us sick – we are just missing the right antioxidants. The juice cleanses. The fasts or the cheat meals. In reality, we are all ill from a loss of community, a loss of social safety nets and the general psychological erosion that comes from spending too much time online. This is probably me talking waaaaaay above my pay grade, but it doesn't feel coincidental that we turn to people who behave obsessively and compulsively in response to the gnawing anxiety of the modern world. People who seem to make sense of the world (even though it makes *no* sense) by putting things in their correct places. It's the pursuit of order in a disordered world all over again, and the only people who seem to have solutions are those who are obsessed with order.

I should add that I am really not trying to shame people with

In reality, we are all ill from a loss of community, a loss of social safety nets and the general psychological erosion that comes from spending too much time online.

genuine compulsive disorders. There are many incredible people who have used the Internet for good (*The Internet? For good?*) and really opened up conversations about neurodiversity and mental health by sharing their experiences of the world and their mind. Such people are a positive force in our society, but others who present obsessive control and order as being 'healthy' or 'clean' for attention on the Internet are a negative for everyone, whether they are neurotypical or not.

This is all quite heavy, and these are all the types of things that people with far more expertise and qualifications than me should be discussing, but I'm on social media, so I get to be one of the solutions, apparently. My solution is that disorder and imperfection are fine. Being unhealthy sometimes doesn't make you impure, and colour-coding your life is not required for you to have a hope of having your shit together. I also really *have* to say that men on the Internet who performatively iron their bed sheets are probably psychopaths. SORRY I'VE BEEN TRYING SO HARD NOT TO SAY IT. I wanted to seem distant and unprejudiced and not shamey but there are literally millions of people turning to Hannibal Lecter Jrs for life advice and it's messed up. We are messed up. I think what might be *most* messed up is that the majority of the people we watch doing this stuff are probably *pretending*. The whole 'I'm Hannibal Lecter Jr, I iron my bed sheets' is an act, it's cosplay and about as real as 'productive daily routines' because, if these guys are making swans out of towels to put on their beds and hoovering the air outside their house, they'll be doing it *all day and for ever.* They can do nothing else. Someone will have to stage an intervention.

'Dr, all he does is film himself ironing, hoovering and exercising.'

'Sounds like a great young man.'

'What?'

'Great young man. Sounds clean, healthy and productive. Heart emoji.'

'Er... Doctor, are you maybe on Instagram? Like... a lot?'

'Hehehe, how could you tell?'

...

'Get me a different doctor.'

Which, of course, you won't be able to do, as we've outsourced all our healthcare to private contractors and all our bedside manner to people who make juices on the Internet. It's a really terrible irony that (particularly in the UK and USA) our most recent governments (OK, USA – *all* governments) have neglected healthcare, while people on the Internet have risen to take on the mantle of health communicators. We used to get health advice from a doctor when we needed it, a few times a year, and now we can see health advice all the time but none of the doctors.

Which is OK, apparently, because humanity has discovered smoothies and the gym. Yes, the gym, which is like the Batcave of the Internet, where all the real work that gives influencers their superpowers takes place. Why? Because being in good shape, lean and muscular, is the ONE thing that unites influencers across every category in this book. Food influencer? Abs. Showing off your spare kids' playhouse? Abs. Travelling the world with the one you love. Abs. Social media is just one big thirst trap where the models pretend to care about different things (like health or ice), and the people watching constantly pretend to care about the health or ice more than the abs. We know it's the abs, people. The jig is up. Admit it.

It is because of this that I have some grudging respect for the fitness influencers. They are the only ones who admit that people basically just want to look at nice bodies on the Internet. They do slow-mo videos of butt workouts and don't bat an eyelid, they zoom in on a lat or ab and only sometimes pretend that they are doing it to make you more productive. They are the last vestige of honesty on social media.

Except for when they are not. The most obvious example is when they manipulate time. You see, a 'fitness transformation' on the Internet takes about 30 seconds. In reality, it takes about 30 months of working out for an hour nearly every day. I know I'm being a bit harsh here, as some of them may have tried to upload a 1,000-hour workout transformation video and just couldn't find the storage or audience but, as a rule, the sped-up nature of Internet fitness seems like it is distorting our perspective. It's good to be fit, but it is important to know that it takes a lot of time and effort, and looking at a speeded-up video of people doing bum crunches[2] is not going to get you any closer to having a godlike physique. In fact, watching videos in general isn't going to make you any healthier. It's definitely good to have some information and to be informed, but I would guess that most people who decide to get into fitness probably watch more videos about it than they really need to, when they could simply go for a walk instead.

I just don't think watching a video, buying a workout plan or subscribing to a weekly shipment of supplements is going to have any more effect than moving around but,

---

[2] Is that a thing? Can you tell I don't bum crunch often?

unfortunately for the Internet, moving around is free. This is why there is such a focus on supplements across social media. Proprietary blends of adaptogens and things that end in -ine can be sold for lots of money by people who have done all of the moving around while you have watched them. There is a supplement for everything, so many, in fact, that you wonder why we ever bothered with food because clearly it doesn't work.

Which will be great news to the many people who profit from diet advice on the Internet. This is a big industry, powered by the sadness generated when online thirst merchants met a broken food culture. It honestly feels sometimes like the Internet, food producers and private healthcare providers are in cahoots, trying to make us both unhealthy and self-loathing. Process the food, make people hate themselves and get rid of free healthcare while distracting people with influencers telling them that they need to try a juice fast. I know, I went a bit political there, but this is my shot so I'm going to take it. If you live in the UK, fight for the NHS. People in other countries die every day because basic medical provisions are too expensive, while in the UK you can have life-saving surgery and not pay a penny after the fact. You don't have to pay to give birth. We have created something amazing that we need to take care of, and we need to be careful not to be so distracted by 'wellness' influencers that we forget about the need for proper healthcare, and the beauty of a system that offers it to everyone, regardless of their economic circumstances.

Of course, I'm not saying that the Internet and medicine are always on completely opposite sides. There are amazing people like Dr Rena Malik (@RenaMalikMD), Dr Idrees Mughal (@dr_idz), Dr Hazel Wallace (@thefoodmedic) and

Dr Ranj (@drranj), who combine the rigours of medical practice with the reach that social media provides, and I am glad that they are there. We need to appreciate them and their free advice, just as we need to appreciate affordable healthcare systems. When the Internet is a vehicle for experts to share their knowledge, it can be a beautiful thing.

Which is nice, because the rest of the time it seems to be a vehicle for idiots to share videos of their beautifully organised kitchens. Yes, we've left the hot topic of NHS privatisation to move on to the much colder one of fridges and ice cubes. I hope I have been clear enough about my reasons for tying together Internet health culture and cleanliness/organisation for that not to be too odd a segue. So shall we begin our chat about organisation and cleanliness with a little test? It is a great opportunity for you to begin your application to povodemia (meant like a povvo academic, but sounds like some sort of outbreak so it might be best to drop it from here on).

Why is there so much content on the Internet about transferring foods from branded to clear containers?[3]

Is it:

1 a neurotic desire for order in a disordered world
2 a way for people whose most marketable talents/ personalities are their kitchens to thrive
3 the Kardashians?

If you said number 1, then well done. You've been reading closely and your comprehension skills are good. If you said number 2, I love your cattiness and I agree. Ice

---

[3] When we literally already have problems with *too much* packaging.

cubes are not a profession.[4] If you said number 3, and 'The Kardashians' isn't just your answer for every trivia question you ever face,[5] then, well done, that's nice knowledge, but you didn't do quite as well as your classmates who said 'All of the above.'

Yes, it's all of them, with the Kardashians being the most niche answer, so it's the one that we'll dwell on. I don't know if it's actually true, but I have been told that the transferring trend – or the 'Pantry Restock' to those of you who speak TikTok – is a result of the need for greater control over product placement in the show *Keeping Up with the Kardashians*. As I say, I can't be 100 per cent sure that's true, but the following explanation sounds 100 per cent plausible to me. Due to the ridiculous number of brand partnership deals that the show had going on, it became difficult for those working on the show to guarantee that the only products ever shown would be those from companies that had a deal in place. It meant that, from time to time, a label would be shown which was a rival of a product that the show had been paid to advertise. To avoid this TERRIBLE confusion, it was agreed that everything would be decanted into neutral containers, with only those products that were on the partnership list kept in their branded packaging. This proceeded to create a whole new corner of the Internet. Unintentionally. You have to give the family credit: it can create a massive online industry out of *trying not to brand things*.

So, apparently, once the Kardashians started moving

---

[4] Unless you work in an ice cube factory.
[5] As in:
Who signed the Declaration of Independence?
Kourtney, Khloé, Kim.

certain products into clear containers, others decided it was time to follow, and they achieved pretty great results. The combination of ASMR, organisation and subtle product placement created a heady brew that viewers couldn't get enough of and brands loved. It appears that the only thing better than someone saying, 'I eat *this* cereal brand' (which sounds like an advert) is saying, 'I love moving *this* cereal brand into this container' (which just sounds like the tinkling of cereal on glass). It pretends to be about the container when really it is about the cereal. Pretty clever actually.

Even if it is really odd. There is a brilliant article by Kelly Prendergast (2023) in which she dissects the trend for pantry restocks and transferring videos. She notes a few really interesting things. The first is that homes and kitchens have been places of work for women (and sometimes men) for centuries, whether this was farming, weaving, piecework or the domestic work involved in preparing meals, cleaning and looking after a family, but these videos transform kitchens and pantries into a whole new kind of workspace. The people in them are working to make them look like retail environments. They present food as though it is for sale. Khloé Kardashian's pantry is that of someone who, as one poster put it, 'worships a retail environment rather than someone who desires a home'. That's what the pantries of TikTok look like to me – little personal shops owned by the person who stocks them. The branding is removed to be replaced by the branding of the person who posted the video – which is whatever choice of neutral packaging they desire. It is adding another step to the retail chain.

In this way, Prendergast argues, the kitchen restock video shows work, work that follows the logic of an Amazon warehouse. The kitchen and pantry are transformed into perfectly operational, ordered spaces, which seem like they could be run by a computer rather than a busy cook. So the kitchen restocker becomes both shop owner and warehouse manager, while also running a reality TV series about their warehouse/shop.

At no point do they need to cook. This is quite a common theme because actual cooking is too messy to fit the brief of 'kitchen' content. Think about it, no one decants tinned plum tomatoes into another container, but they will sure as darn move some ice cubes around. Ice cubes are clean and controlled, they are food without food (except maybe some little flowers or berries frozen in) and they allow people to present the feeling of a kitchen without any of the hot messiness that comes from actually cooking. Ice cubes are also something you can manipulate, flavour and shape without having to cook. You freeze, which is cooking in reverse.

They are also the ultimate symbol of having *waaaaay* too much time on your hands. Ice cubes are, beyond cooling things, nearly completely unnecessary. You might take some time to make a few ice cubes if you have done with the shopping and cooking, cleaning and working, socialising and learning, but to dedicate time, money and thought to something that adds nearly no quality to your life is a sign of how free you are, and how much spare money and time you have. I think they are also popular because they are impermanent. Ice cubes literally melt away. You are saying, 'I have time and money to put into something that will disappear, because time and money are nothing to me.' The final selling point of the ice cube, of course, is that they are the lowest-calorie edible-looking thing. They look like Haribo but influencer moms can actually consume them. Nice, brightly coloured things that catch the light in interesting ways but won't get in the way of your quest for ABS! ABS! ABS! And they're not branded, so no worries about getting in the way of your partnerships.

Until now that is. I've done so many videos taking the piss out of icefluencers that people have been requesting that I bring out a range. I don't know if that's too meta. Will people even get that I'm in on the joke? The cubes might have to spell the words 'THIS ICE SIGNIFIES THAT I'M NOT POOR' or something like that but, even so, I think it might be going too far. You would also need a lot of room in your freezer for all those letters and, because you're batch-cooking and storing 1,000 years of stew[6] in there, that might not be possible. You are also probably failing to order your fridge and freezer with the efficiency that the Internet expects of you, so you will have no hope of storing the three ice-cube trays necessary to spell out 'WHAT ON GOD'S GREEN EARTH ARE THESE?' (28 letters).

'Why don't you just pay someone to do it? Or get a robot butler?' These are the sorts of solutions that povvos clearly haven't thought of yet because, if we had, we'd be as clean and organised as the influencers we are told to admire. I hope we are all in agreement that these kitchen and pantry influencers must have a whole heap of paid help. There is no way they have houses that big, fridges that organised and time enough to film themselves organising stuff in a big house without some domestic support. I want to see the cleaners' videos. They would produce proper, useful content on how to clean a house that is five times too big in under an hour, alongside a few straight-to-camera pieces about

---

6 The unsuccessful follow-up to *One Hundred Years of Solitude*.

how concerned they are about the man who irons the bed and how she secretly has to make the towel swans.

A boy can dream, but I don't think we'll be seeing that content upgrade in our feeds any time soon. It would be more informative, more entertaining and more representative of life in the West today than anything else on social media, but it would also probably not help to sell much tat – and what would the Internet be without the subtle sale of tat? Nothing. It takes skill, invention and poise and it's deeply annoying. The way people sell stuff these days is enough to make you pine for the golden age of advertising. By which I mean Barry Scott in the Cillit Bang adverts. If you don't know who Barry Scott is, you are either very young or very good at leaving behind the memory of burst eardrums because, if you were alive in 2004, Barry Scott shouting, 'Hi, I'm Barry Scott!' should be singed on to your brain. (You may, of course, not be from a country that actually sells Cillit Bang so – like the very young – have zero idea what I am talking about, but trust me when I say, Barry Scott shouted loud enough that you could probably have heard the echo of his voice wherever in the world you call home.)

Now, when I say, 'If you don't know who Barry Scott is', I need you to understand that *no one* knows who Barry Scott is, other than that he was the man who shouted 'Hi, I'm Barry Scott!' like we should know who he was. It was quite confusing. Anyway, the most confusing part (I've just looked it up) is that Barry Scott was played by an actor. So the one thing we know about the man who said, 'Hi, I'm Barry Scott' (that he was Barry Scott) is actually completely untrue. At this point, the shouting is all that remains. And the blatant sexism. I just rewatched one of the ads online, and the opening line is that 'Over a million women across the UK are

at it.[7] They've replaced their multipurpose cleaners wiiiith...
Cillit Bang Universal Degreaser.' It was another time, not
really that long ago but, culturally and technologically, it was
another era. Shouty men only sell shouty men things these
days on the Internet, whereas your modern equivalents of
Cillit Bang are sold with quiet whispers, by wispy women in
wispy dresses online.

Which is funny because cleaning is not something that
really changes by era, while the way we sell the idea of it
keeps transforming. My mum still has a vacuum cleaner from
the 1970s. Dyson was just a hippy with a dream (of suction)
when she got it, yet it still lasts and still does the same things
it was supposed to then. It hoovers. It doesn't have voice
controls or an automatic setting that you control remotely
with an app, but it hoovers. It has outlasted Barry Scott, and
the overt sexism of the Cillit Bang adverts, because cleaning
hasn't changed, even if the ways we talk about it have. So
here is the first tip: **don't fall for cleaning fads and fast-
tech.** Povvos have been clean for hundreds of years now
and it's not hand-held or robot hoovers that have done it. It's
having access to water, a hoover and enough time to clean.
So hold on to your heirloom hoover, forget about subscriptions
for laundry tablets and keep it old-fashioned. The old ways
are the good ways, just not in the case of Cillit Bang.

The second suggestion harks back to some of the advice
that was included in Chapter 4, about fashion: **reuse old
clothes as cleaning rags.** It is a testament to our versatility
that, in the middle of a Venn diagram marked both 'fashion'
and 'cleaning rags', we find ourselves. We are fashionable,
but not too fashionable for rags. Our clothes are nice, but

---

7 Bad joke that.

from the rag trade they came and to rags they shall return. This is great, and a good motivator not to buy anything that feels too expensive to ever become a rag (after it is downgraded from outside clothes, to home clothes, to pyjamas). It may spend a period of time as workout wear, if you are not too bothered about being dressed in matching Sweaty Betty and are of the jogging persuasion. I fluctuate. Sometimes I do actually try to get fit, sometimes it just doesn't happen. I'm not going to try and persuade you either way, though, but I will pass on some advice from the gang about being fit the povvo way.

Do it outside. Because not every attempt to raise our heart rate has to sound like an Ibiza classics night. Exercise doesn't have to take place in the dark, and it doesn't have to cost loads of money. These are three things that the fitness industry wants you to believe are essential for health but, deep down, we know they're not true. So free yourself from the social pressures that the exercise industry profits from. You can be sweaty without a club soundtrack. Jumping around alone in the park does not *necessarily* make you seem deranged. A long walk *is* exercise. You do not have to spend £40 a month to get shouted at by someone who IS SO FIT THAT THEY ARE NOT EVEN SWEATING FROM THE WORKOUT THEY ARE LEADING. So do it on your own terms, in a place you are free to be. It may make you feel a bit self-conscious for a

Free yourself from the social pressures that the exercise industry profits from. You can be sweaty without a club soundtrack.

time but, remember, anyone who judges you for exercising in a rag, in the park is not our kind of person. They are probably just as hard on themselves, and their wallet.

Speaking of wallets, fillemup as you get fit by **moving around at work, because you have an actual job.** Hard one to believe, this. Judging from the world of productivity and the fitness community, you would think we were all necessarily sedentary and need to be shouted at on a bike to achieve anything approaching movement, but actually having a job can require you to move around a lot. You're getting *paid* to get fit. That's more like it! Be grateful that the floor manager asked you to move a load of boxes up to the store counter or a patient is having a cardiac arrest on floor 9 of the building and the lift is broken.[8]

If your job is quite a sit-down affair and you would like to feel healthier, don't be afraid to just walk up and down the stairs every hour or so. Or tap your feet to the music on your headphones while you finish that spreadsheet. Fidgeting is good for you, no matter what they told you at school.

Take **natural remedies.** No, I'm not a COVID conspiracist and, no, I'm not gonna try to tell you that cow's piss is the secret to glossier skin. I just mean, like, normal stuff. Obviously healthy stuff that old Asian women might know about. Ginger. Fresh mint. Hibiscus. Don't worry that some of these plants have been caught up in the woo-woo cycle and weaponised by people pretending to be hippies for likes. There are reasons that they were considered healthy foods *before* they were considered supplements... It's because they are healthy foods. With that in mind, I regret calling them natural remedies – they are just healthy foods. So eat some healthy foods. Which

---

[8] Don't actually be grateful for the cardiac arrest bit, though, of course.

leads us on to the next suggestion.

Eat mostly plants. Frozen ones are really cheap and last. Pretty simple that, but I hear it's good advice. We are told that cheap food is processed food and vice versa, but it's not true – plants can always be cheap. So make your kid like salad. Make yourself like salad. And beans. I hate to rely on old Asian women as a justification again, but if they could feed large families on pulses, plants and the odd bit of meat sometimes, you can feed yourself on a chickpea curry. This might require you to... **learn to cook.**

Annoying, I know. It's like homework. You didn't buy this book for advice that would make your life harder. Well, good news. If you can't already cook, this tip will only make your life harder for a short time while you're learning, then much easier once you have. The truth is that cooking is made to seem much more difficult than it really is by the millions of cookbooks and foodfluencers out there. You don't *have* to follow complicated recipes. Your first attempt in the kitchen doesn't *have* to involve a dinner party and six Ottolenghi recipes. You can start out with ingredients that you understand. Once you get into your stride, you will *definitely* save money, and be healthier.

So make that chickpea curry and, beforehand, **use full tins as exercise weights.** This is such a legitimate tip that it does make me wonder why people ever *buy* weights. Things being heavy is supposed to be an issue, a problem that you avoid, yet people pay for it nowadays. I can understand people *maaaaybe* buying something that is like 20kg and hand-held, but really for anything under 5kg, tins really have to be the answer. Just Sellotape chickpea tins together and up the reps if you want to get really hench.

The final suggestion is to **block toxic people on**

socials. Blocking is free, and the shits you give should never become a renewable resource, so exercise your right to block. While you're at it, unfollow all the social media accounts that gave you nonsense info you didn't follow.

Health *is* wealth. But, by stealth, our health has become *their* wealth, so try something ealth. Wear rags to the park and do squat supersets with Sellotaped chickpea tins because you're juiced up on ginger. Don't be self-conscious – that's what the healthfluencers want.

BEG YOUR PAR
ROUND BALLY IC
RICH, YOU'RE PC
SPOKEN LIKE A
POVVO, BECAUS
NOT AN ANIMAL
WHY?, BECAUSE
YOU'RE A POVV
WHAT ON GOD'S
EARTH, ON TODA
EPISODE OF..., R
SISTER SHERRIE
HAVE A DAY OFF
GASP, STOP IT

PETS AND PARENTING

WHAT ON GOD'S GREEN EARTH IS A BABY SPRINKLE?

To all the parents out there, I apologise for the suggestion that I am comparing your children to pets. To all you pet owners out there, I apologise for the suggestion that I am comparing your pets to children. If you've got both, then I just hope you are OK and, remember, you will sleep again *someday*.

Joking aside, I hope you can understand why I have paired these two subjects together. It's because while, in the real world, there are clearly differences between owning a pet and parenting a child, on social media, they are effectively the same thing. They are bubbly little devices that showcase our humanity, struggle to behave for photos and produce far more bodily fluids than anyone ever admits.

They are also both often cute, and we've been over how important cuteness is on the Internet. Sex may sell, but cuteness *engages*... then sells even more. If you can be sexy and have access to something cute, then, my word, you can be rich. You will, of course, at that point have achieved the sexy–rich–cute triumvirate and probably hate this book. I plead with you not to use your vast resources to destroy my small semblance of a reputation. Or turn Blackburn into a puppy farm out of spite. Or whatever it is you want to do. You sexy, pug-toting supervillain.

Maybe people don't get pets or have children *just* to raise their engagement. Maybe there is a more wholesome reason. If you were sent as much Internet nonsense as I am, though (it's my job, keep it coming), you would struggle to think differently too. From what I can see, the whole timeline of parenting and pet ownership is a choreographed stunt on the Internet. It is a vehicle for expressing the kindness and wealth that you don't extend to commoners. A way to show that you will flash cash and express love if the person or thing you are giving it to is entirely dependent on you. I want to see someone throw a rich kid party for children at the food bank rather than for their mini-me. Or give a homeless person's pet a velour tracksuit and makeover. I want the Internet's show-offs to offer other people's pets and children a fraction of the performative love that they do to their own.

Because there is a lot of performative love. There are gender reveals. Baby showers. Birthdays. Pet get-togethers and profiles written in the first person by puppies. There is a lot of appetite for people doing seemingly selfless, loving things on the Internet. Now I want them to do it for people and dogs who aren't already set to inherit fortunes.

It's unlikely, though, and it may be that people on the Internet have realised the best way to guarantee their child's inheritance is to start building them a social media brand when they are a child or, preferably, *before* they are even born. People who have been smart enough to be extremely rich already and monetise their love can move seamlessly into monetising their embryo. Now that's what I call a good start in life, and if that child's Insta keeps growing as they do, they may not even *need* an inheritance. So it is best to start with a gender reveal video. This is what used to be called 'looking at an unborn child's crotch'. This did not translate well into content, so when medical science advanced enough for a baby's biological sex to become visible on scans, a whole new world of engagement opened up. 'What to expect when you were expecting' became 'lots of likes'.

The basic logic of an elite online gender reveal video is that you have to present either the colour blue or pink (very progressive) in a surprising way, while also letting people know that you are very rich. This could take the form of having the interior of your unnecessarily large Bentley relined in blue, letting off fireworks near a large, dry wooded area or flying a plane overhead emitting colourful trails. You may want to spray-paint your 14th-century Ming vase. It doesn't matter quite how you do it, as long as you can showcase your wealth while paying some lip service to the new life you are creating.

You will then have a bit of a content lull until after the birth. I know, it's really hard not to monetise your unborn child for that long, but just hold out because there will be so many chances to show off later. You can at least cash in on the baby shower.[1] Traditionally, these were events where women in a community would come together to share knowledge and resources that a new mother would benefit from. It was a way of recycling know-how and bibs that was entirely wholesome and in no way profitable. That obviously had to change. So now we have what are effectively gatherings to show off expensive baby equipment – £98,000 diamond-encrusted rocking horse, £40,0000 rose gold pram, £640 Tiffany baby cup (if you are the CHEAP friend). These are really beautiful, social events because not only can you showcase your wealth and the love in your heart, but your friends can, too, by trying to upstage one another with even more unnecessarily diamond-encrusted things. Truly, we have reached the end of days, and the baby is not even born yet.

Once it is, the bonanza can begin.[2] A baby is a great addition to the influencer collective (previously known as 'a family'), because there are now whole new styling and

---

[1] Or baby sprinkle. Apparently, a second baby (and any more after that) gets a baby sprinkle.

[2] Apparently, you can expect a 'push present'. A Rolls-Royce or something.

photography opportunities that open up. Whereas previously the influencers only had themselves to dress, they now have a miniature version of themselves to clothe too. The fashion industry has been quick to move on this, given that they simply have to make the same expensive clothes with half the fabric and charge the same (if only they had been so flexible about plus-size ranges). I would hazard a guess that about 20 per cent of the world's most expensively dressed people are children, and, again, this is fantastic news for the fashion industry as children need new clothes *all the time*. Like their

◀◀ ▶▶

I would hazard a guess that about 20 per cent of the world's most expensively dressed people are children, and, again, this is fantastic news for the fashion industry as children need new clothes *all the time*.

parents. They are perfect little consumers because they don't have a clue what is going on, but require a wardrobe overhaul at least every six months.

Then there is the key decision over whether to match or not. People on social media with a great variety of clothes seem to take inexplicable joy from making their children wear the same outfit as them – like they are a big group of overpaid/underworked Power Rangers. While you might expect them to take advantage of the opportunity to dress someone else in different expensive clothes, narcissism seems to trump variety as, quite regularly, the children are in the same clothes as their parents. This is obviously a bit creepy and may end up on the long list of subjects these children might share with a therapist in 20 years' time, in a conversation[3] that maybe will begin something like this.

'Hi, Doctor.'

'Hi, Apple.'[4]

'That's not my name.'

'Sorry, that's someone else. Hi Moroccan.'[5]

'I'm not called that either.'

'Oh no, I was just saying hi to that Moroccan person over there.'

'Oh. Isn't it a bit odd to refer to them just by their nationality?'

'Don't worry. Anyway, how are you, X-ZAI?'[6]

'I don't call myself that any more.'

'OK, what do you call yourself?'

'X-ZAII.'

'OK, hi…'

'But most people just call me Alan.'

After this long delay (the therapist is a bit odd, but I expect them to be), they can get into the nitty-gritty of their childhood.

'Yeah, so I'm just really trying to process some things from my childhood.'

'That's good. What have you been thinking about?'

---

[3] An entirely imaginary and intentionally ridiculous scenario (if you're famous and planning to sue).

[4] Paltrow and Martin.

[5] Carey and Cannon.

[6] I can only assume we're just a few celebrity baby name cycles away from this name given that Elon Musk actually called his child X Æ A-XII.

'Well, it all started with the time four million people celebrated me having male sex organs by watching a blue aeroplane roll out of a hanger.'

'Hmmm, yes, and how did that make you feel?'

'I wasn't born.'

'Yes, but how did it make you feel when you processed it?'

'I've already said that I wasn't born, so I feel like it was sort of odd.'

Now, unfortunately, the therapist also works with Alan/X-ZAII's parents, so doesn't want to admit that it *was* entirely odd. Plus, the therapist is making $600,000 and plans to do their own gender reveal next week. So they try to smooth over this past trauma and move on to more manageable things, like, 'I had to wear a uniform as a child – I only wore whatever my dad was wearing' or 'My fourth birthday was sponsored by Hermès and livestreamed on OnlyFans.'[7] You know, normal childhood things. Normal because everything from the gender reveal to weirdly extravagant birthdays seems to have been normalised.

Whole houses get converted into party spaces and the editorial team from the *Barbie* movie probably get paid overtime to make a supercut of the festivities. The birthday child has to pose a lot, when all they really want is to put crayons in their nose and eat cake until they are sick. In between poses they may be allowed to engage in some on-brand fun that doesn't risk ruining their outfit before the presents get given/filmed. This is obviously another chance to share joy and exhibit wealth, so must be taken very seriously. Wealthy friends of the wealthy people can give

---

[7] *Before* it was mostly naked people, jeez.

gifts that show their wealth and, at times, appreciation of the four-year-old who is having this party thrust on them. They might choose to give them a £600 Balenciaga lunchbox, maybe a £500 Gucci pencil case or the £260 one, without pencils, if they are cheap. Or they might decide to get the small child a $1.5 million diamond-encrusted Rubik's cube, which they won't like, and, even if they did, they wouldn't be allowed to twist round because it would make the diamonds look all wrong. This is the life of the child in the diamond-encrusted cage. It does not necessarily look like a happy one, and I'm sure if we could only get in touch with the parents, we might be able to spread the costs of this single party across about 10,000 parties that kids actually enjoy, kids whose parents can't afford a party at all. You just need some cake and enough space for kids to run around in circles. That's about it.

In my opinion, the Kardashian kids' parties are the epitome of expensive and unnecessary (*expencessary?*). They are expensive because they will really follow through on a chosen theme, seemingly even changing the colour of the carpet (*karpet?*) to match the party theme (Bonner, 2023), and unnecessary because the parties are for events like first day at school (Jones, 2023). Speaking as a teacher, it is notable but not something to party about. Some celebs do it quite well. I have to give some credit to DJ Khaled, for example, as he appears to throw some parties that *are* expensive, but fun, and at times when you should actually have parties. Like his son's birthday. I may not think that he has the best music (no matter what he says) but DJ Khaled does throw the best five-year-old's birthday party. *Sponsored by Papa John's Pizza* (@asadkhaled, 2021). I kid you not. You may be wondering why I know about DJ Khaled's son's fifth birthday party, and that would be reasonable. It is, in fact, because he has had his own Instagram page since pretty much the day he was born, and he and I are jostling in the followers charts. His posts are all written in the first person, and have been since before he could write (last week?), but this doesn't stop odd and arguably not very intelligent people from thinking it is actually him. Messages such as, 'Memories last a lifetime God bless you and your beautiful family @ djkhaled let us certify you in case of an emergency for CPR we love you!' from RestoreHeartCPr are at the less odd end of the spectrum, while 'Happy Belated @asahdkhaled, your dad @djkhaled was lucky person have you. Btw, can u say to your beloved father to let me message him through DM @ email?' from malaysian_coach_4_real_atkins. That is at the odder end. Obviously, Malaysian Coach believes that this five-year-old is running the page and editing the videos, while also having his dad's ear when it comes to organising real Atkins. It is, of course, not OK to message random five-year-olds on the Internet, whether or not you are a coach_4_real.

Anyway, I personally think that Khaled's son's Instagram is one of the better ones among the other five-year-olds' accounts on there. His parties have go-karts and pizza sponsorship (save that dough), and the editing of the online videos actually seems to lean into the craziness that this kind of event should be based on. There is no posing, and there should never be.

People in the entertainment industry say 'never work with children or animals'[8] and I think that is because posing

---

[8] Unless you're Beyoncé, then you get your 11-year-old (in 2023) on stage every night (Bowenbank, 2023).

doesn't come naturally to either. Strangely, people in the industry or otherwise in the public eye have somehow neglected to take the obvious stance in response to this rule, which is 'don't make children or animals work', in entertainment or otherwise. It is saying a lot that it is the *difficulty* of working with them that they home in on, rather than the *immorality* of putting children and pets to work.[9] The pets at least don't know they are working. They may wonder why they have been put in a tiara that says third birthday on it, but if I know French Bulldogs, then I would assume they are not aware of the concept of a tiara or the need to try to look smouldering.

Maybe I'm old-fashioned. Maybe these pets do understand everything that is being asked of them, and see it as a fair trade-off for having their own pet mansion affixed to the house their humans live in. Maybe they see themselves as employed. Fashionistas. There is no denying that some of those pugs are better dressed than I am, and many of them have larger bedrooms, so who's the mug really? Me, but maybe them as well, because I get the sense that, like the children of richfluencers, the pets would rather be leading a more old-school, muddy existence. They don't want to be vegan, tiaras are uncomfortable and

> **There is no denying that some of those pugs are better dressed than I am, and many of them have larger bedrooms, so who's the mug really?**

---

[9] As influencers. Guide dogs, rescue dogs, fire investigation dogs – I get that, they like that stuff more than posing.

they already have coats on.[10] If they knew what it was, I'm sure they most certainly wouldn't want to be cloned.

Huh? Cloned? You've gone a bit sci-fi there, Shabaz. I know, but so has the world. People clone their pets. Barbra Streisand did it (Petter, 2019) and now I can only assume that petfluencers will follow, in the hope of achieving true consistency. If you have a pet that is popular with your followers, why let that be interrupted by something so ick as the circle of life? I'll tell you why, because the poor dog has to spend the last year of its life WATCHING ITS OWN CLONE GROW TOWARDS ITS PRIME. Can you imagine that? Can you picture the torment you would feel as you struggle into your old age and LITERAL YOU bounds in, full of the exuberance of youth. *You* wants to play with *you.* You do, too, but you are too old for *you.* You just don't have the vivacity you used to – *that you* has it now. *You* gradually replaces you in photos. You would put up a fight, but you know that *you* would win, so you stand no chance. Maybe, though, just maybe, you know *your* weaknesses. Maybe you can use your intricate knowledge of your old self to set a trap for *your new self.* You always used to try to run after the postie, when you heard the letters arrive. Maybe you can time it just right, so *that you* gets locked out, or, better, run over.

You succeed.

But the next morning, there is just *another* you, waiting to take over from *that you.*

And Mum's upped the security.

That is, of course, a terrifying and terrible situation (which I am I now planning to make into a film). It is also

---

10 Can you imagine being forced to wear a gilet on top of your coat?

the lived experience of some dogs. I only hope that the old dogs learn some new tricks, such as becoming comfortable with the passage of time and finding joy in watching their younger selves grow. Or else descend into a brutal and long-lasting series of murders that gives them purpose until their dying day.

I thought it was only cats that had nine lives.

Cats occupy a very different place on the Internet from dogs. I think they are used far less by influencers because they are not as dependent or malleable as dogs. Cats simply won't do what they are told, so don't get to be part of the influencer family quite as often as dogs. To me, they are more like a cantankerous aunt or lesser-seen cousin, swinging by every once in a while when it suits them. Cats are independently funny, while dogs fit the bill much more by being amusingly dependent. You see, cats are the main characters in their own show. They may appear online for doing battle with a robot hoover or sometimes jumping over very high things, but they are rarely willing to be accessories. They are intelligent enough to add real character to the influencer experience, but too independent to offer a reliable stream of content.

A rabbit, mouse or rat is dependent enough, but lacks personality. Sorry, rat people, I am not saying your rat is not a star, but it might just lack the tools to help you build an online brand. If, though, like most healthy people, you have no intention of co-opting another life in the name of developing a brand, then, please, have a rat. Be my guest. Rat away. In fact, I am so supportive of your rat goals that I am going to make it the first of our povvo tips in this chapter: **get a rat.** Rats are low maintenance, and high-functioning pets. They are clever (I have heard stories of rats working out how to open the treats cupboard), but cheap and resourceful. Rats can pretty much pay their own way, as anyone who has lived in a major city can see. So, yeah, get a rat. It's the right thing to do. If you are more old school, or still buy into the anti-rat propaganda, you could get a gerbil or a hamster. Because a gerbil is not just for childhood. These, again, are a cheap, fun way to own a pet without spending loads of money.

As is **owning a pet rock.** I'm serious. It was a thing. It is the cheapest pet on the market and has a lot going for it that other pets simply don't have. Who else can say that their pet is four billion years old? Or that it was born in a volcano? Surely only dark wizards who chose their pet because it was a four-billion-year-old superbeing that was forged at the centre of the earth. And who cares about them? Amirite?

If you would like something slightly more animate than a rock (you poser), but easier to insure than an English Bulldog, you can't go wrong with a **Tamagotchi.** They *are* pets. They ARE. And they give you some of the pet experience without any of the waste, long-term costs or genuine interactions.

You may be committed to genuine interactions. You may want to live with something more complex than a hand-held Japanese toy from 1995, so if you are *incredibly high maintenance* like that, then we should consider how you can actually make having a normal pet or child less expensive. Your povvo smart start should begin at the point of purchase. It should be clear that I am talking about a *pet* here, not a child. We do not purchase children.[11] **Do not get sucked into buying a pedigree.**[12] Yes, they look nice and, yes, it is

----

[11] They're too expensive. Joke.
[12] Pet rocks with pedigree, though, are encouraged. Pet rocks have incredible pedigrees. Igneous rock's family tree stretches back 4.6 billion years. Pure.

charming to be able to say that your dog has a pure, high-class lineage (so at least *someone* in the house does) but, really, this is both expensive and superficial. There are lots of animals without homes, so if you have the experience and understanding, then foster or adopt a pet. It is both nearly free and provides a home for a being in need. If you feel that you do not have the experience to support an adopted pet, because often they are traumatised and need genuine support, then simply go for a mutt. There are people out there who are not breeding dogs for money – they just had some puppies the old-fashioned way – and you can get a sweet, genetically diverse, puppy that doesn't cost a grand or more.

If you really put in the time to make that mutt a capable, functioning member of society, then it can be a friend, a family member and, at some point, a *carer*: **let the pets take care of the kids.** I've had this suggestion a few times and it sounds legit. I would have more trust in a capable Labrador cross to take care of an eight-year-old than I would in myself. This means you can save on childcare or just be free to go for a wee in peace for once, so I give it the star of approval, even if it is terrible advice.[13] If you have high-falootin' ideas about the childcare staff you employ, you can **get the older kids to take care of the younger ones.** This is, of course, a staple of povvo communities worldwide and it can be a great option. You do have to commit to having more than one child and keeping a reasonable age gap between them (this book does not promote four-year-olds being left to manage one-year-olds), but if you can make it work, it is really a beautiful thing. The coolest thing when

---

13 And a joke.

you are six is a 12-year-old. The most awesome and mature being in the world when you are 12 is 16. Lean into that, you may not be cool to your child, but at least another one of your children could be.

The economies of scale with children and pets are clear to see. They can entertain themselves, so if you are willing to accept that you live in a state of unending chaos with multiple children and animals, then you can at least exist above the chaos because they exist in their own self-regulating ecosystem. I am told this system works best if **you keep them all outdoors.** I know this isn't always an option, but if you have outdoor space, then send the feral pack of dogs and children on their way and, if you don't, then set them loose in a park. They say that nature abhors a vacuum, but your vacuuming abhors the nature of multiple kids and pets, so keep them outdoors as much as possible.

The park is just one of the **free public spaces** that I am told is integral to raising happy, cheap creatures. We have been led to believe that everything has to cost money, that a weekend without a trip to the cinema is wasted, but, in truth, children and animals have been happy in free public spaces for thousands of years, so just don't let them get their standards up. If you bring them up expecting Pizza Express, they will never be happy with a cheese toastie again. Don't let them have linguine before they are 16. Convince them that the park is for every day and cinemas were only created for birthdays. Going out should mean going to free public spaces, so libraries, parks and (the remaining free/cheap) leisure centres are your best friend.

If the free spaces are not an option and the children *have* to be indoors, alternative free fun remains. So many people elaborated on the wonders of **cardboard boxes** for kids and pets that I fear the cardboard marketing board is going to catch wind of it and start jacking up their prices. You do not need a 'cat chaise longue' or a bouncy castle, just get the box that your rich friends' ones came in. This cultivates imagination and frugality in your child or pet and they will genuinely have the time of their lives. If you are creative, you can join in and decorate the boxes, which will probably be more relevant for the child than the cat. Cats are not impressed by cardboard with shells and sequins stuck to it, while children genuinely are.

You do not need a 'cat chaise longue' or a bouncy castle, just get the box that your rich friends' ones came in.

In fact, the incredible imaginations that children have really make them ideal povvos. They do not need hugely expensive toys to do something engaging and interesting. They do not care about brands and, really, they only want *that toy* because someone kept telling them about it. So keep telling them about the toys they *already have* and find ways to spark their imagination around them. On of the best examples of this kind of approach that I have seen is a mother who froze her **children's toys in blocks of ice.** Yes, people, ice content has become relevant, we have gone through the looking glass. She then proceeded to set the toys up in a large bowl and instigate a scenario where all the toys were trapped in some sort of evil icy plot that the children could talk about but had to *wait out* to solve. That is just genius. It is a slow, free, interactive process that will distract children and probably – depending on your particular brand of child – generate far more joy than the

Frozen musical could during those two hours. This is useful, relatable content, particularly if, like me, you plan to own two freezers. I can only imagine the Sunday morning that begins with the children asking where their toys have gone, and you announcing that some sort of icy villain has been in during night. Once they stop crying, the fun can begin and you may genuinely have several hours to yourself to batch-cook a week of meals. We have ice to thank for that.

We also have ice to thank for the arrival of the ice cream van. This technology is only possible thanks to advances in freezing technology and the diligence of people in giant clown cars with speaker systems. As povvos, obviously we need ways to deflect any interest children have in the ice cream van's wares. This is where the line, **'the ice cream van music means they have run out'** comes from. Yes, this may sound sneaky but, if it is necessary, then it must be done. It is the perfect crime as the ice cream van music, although it tries to sound joyful, usually sounds really sad. Now you can add an extra sombre note to the chimes of 'Popeye the sailor man' by creating a myth that it is a sort of funeral march for the lack of ice creams. For there being no Mr Whippy or 99 Flakes. If you can invent a song for when you open the freezer and get out some cheap Neapolitan ice cream, then the circle will be complete.

Yes, your children will have some experiences that are out of step with those of their peers. Yes, they will spend their crawling years with tea towels stuck to their knees to save on leggings and they will think that *Popeye* is actually a *really* sad show, but they will have imagination. They will have insight. Truly, they will be smart, savvy povvos from the day they are born.

Which is surely better than having their own Instagram?

BEG YOUR PAR

ROUND BALLY IO

RICH, YOU'RE PO

SPOKEN LIKE A

POVVO, BECAUS

NOT AN ANIMAL

WHY?, BECAUSE

YOU'RE A POVVO

WHAT ON GOD'S

EARTH, ON TODA

EPISODE OF..., RO

SISTER SHERRIE

HAVE A DAY OFF

GASP, STOP IT

EMPOWERMENT AND MENTAL HEALTH

OH, HAVE A DAY OFF

If you have made it this far, you are probably comfortable with me spouting off about things I am unqualified to discuss. There may have been some uncomfortable moments. You might be a brilliant textile designer who thought I was a bit glib in my criticisms of online fashion. Maybe a van-lifer's Instagram changed your non-van life and you wish I had pulled fewer punches when discussing the vanner community. Maybe your pug's Instagram is actually *really* good. Those are all fair points and, before I begin to discuss a subject that is both above my pay grade and in many ways too delicate to be the subject of (attempted) hilarious takedowns, I must return to some things that I discussed before and say:

- social media is not one thing
- it can be a force for good
- if anything or anyone genuinely makes you happy on social media, they are beyond my criticism, simply because they make you happy.

That kind of relativity is only possible because this book isn't really about social media. It's about us. It's about the fact that this is a new media that involves the observers in a way that no entertainment or information format did before. This involvement has some good points: we can feed back about things we like and dislike and form communities while we are being entertained. It has its bad ones too: because it feels like the content reflects on us personally somehow, it can bring about feelings of guilt or shame. This was not the case with entertainment in the past. No one was watching *Ocean's Eleven* in 2001 and going, 'Jeez, I really need to get my act together if I'm gonna be anything like those guys', or listening to *Woman's Hour* and deciding that the presenter's understanding of feminism somehow made that listener less of a good person. I think, because we are the constituents of social media, because it is made *of us*, we feel like it reflects on us more than anything we have turned to for entertainment or advice before.

Add to this the fact that what social media reflects rarely looks anything like reality. If it *was* making films, they would all be *Ocean's Eleven* or *Eat Pray Love*, without any room for *Kes* or *Trainspotting*. This new(ish) infotainment field that somehow reflects on us is mostly glitzy and glamorous, and that can make us feel pretty crappy for not being able to pull off the largest heist Las Vegas has ever seen (figuratively) or just *be* Julia Roberts. Which is obviously a wild state of affairs. No one saw it coming. There was nothing in our collective experience to turn to when our new media became a giant looking glass, composed of three billion people, which showed us a distorted reflection of a world more perfect than the one we seem to live in. Entertainment used to be entertainment, full stop. No one wanted to know Lady Macbeth's *honest* daily routine.[1] The presenters of the *News at Ten* never claimed to 'Just Wake Up Like This'. We knew that they were actors performing roles.[2] So what I'm saying (arguably a bit late) is that this book is really about the performance of social media, it is about our role in it as observers who become part of the creation by being there and how that can make us feel.

Some of the alternative subtitles I considered for this book get my thinking across:

----

[1] I do actually want to see this now. Could be a great parody channel, imagining the lifestyle Instagrams of figures from history.
[2] Yes, I do think of newsreaders as performers.

- the joy of being ordinary in extraordinary times
- giving the Internet a reality check
- social media for imperfect people
- how I learnt to stop worrying and hate the atomic habits (bit niche that one but a personal fave)
- why no one feels normal on social media
- why we all feel like the odd one out online
- the beauty of life with no filter.

I think the idea of feeling 'like the odd one out online' captures it best. Main character syndrome is rife because everyone is encouraged to make their own reality TV show and, in the process, begins comparing their own staging (appearance) and narrative arc (how interesting their life is) to those of the competition. It's mentally draining, and it's just one of the reasons it's particularly ironic that we get a lot of our mental health advice from social media these days.

I'm not sure there even *was* mental health advice before social media (if there was, I'm not sure it made it to Blackburn). I'm not really sure 'mental health', as it is currently understood, existed before the Internet. There was mental *illness*, and it was approached without enough sympathy or understanding, but there was little idea of wellness, or mental fitness. Now, in part because talking about yourself is one of the best ways to get viewers into your reality show (subscribers to your page), discussions of our psychology have become mainstream. Humans talk to fewer people face to face than they did before but *share* with thousands more online. People also spend more time being openly mean to other people than in the past, but online. As a result, we have people on the Internet telling us about their anxiety, in places dominated by people who are incentivised to say mean things for a reaction. The two must be connected.

I mean, imagine if people in the real world behaved like they do on the Internet. Everyone would be so sad, all the time. You would hardly be able to move without a man with 'Dad. Football fan. Love my country' on his T-shirt telling you that you should go and die in a hole. The 14-year-olds would walk up to you and tell you that you are ugly on a daily basis. The only people you would ever see outside would be wearing a *perfect* face of make-up to go to the shops. Social media is an overwhelmingly beautiful and underwhelmingly mean place a lot of the time, and it is where we go to find motivation and advice for enjoying what can be a cruel world. That is the second irony about mental health and the Internet.

It's not exactly a hot take – 'Newsflash: The Internet Can Make Us Sad'. Neither is it controversial to point out that the last person you need to help you with this problem is someone who wants you to *stay* on the Internet longer. What *is* controversial is that online wellness gurus also can't really talk about money, or wealth inequality as it relates to well-being and mental health, because their content has to be sort of aspirational. The people who succeed in giving this advice on the Internet rarely look broke. As a result, facts about how income, employment and housing relate to mental health incomes almost never come up. The only solutions that are offered are individualistic and ignore big social problems. You should manifest your way to happiness. Meditate. Get a better job. The sad truth is that societal problems are massive drivers of the mental health crisis and no number of individuals on the Internet with individualistic solutions can solve that. Here are some stats based on research from economically developed nations (Mental

Health Foundation, n.d.):

> children in the lowest income quintile... [are] 4.5 times more likely to experience severe mental health problems than those in the highest, suggesting that the income gradient in young people's mental health has worsened considerably over the past decade (Gutman et al., 2015)

> Employment status is linked to mental health outcomes, with unemployed or economically inactive having higher rates of common mental health problems than those employed (Stansfield et al., 2016)

> Those on housing benefit are more than twice as likely to have a common mental health problem than those not receiving it (35.1% vs 14.9%) (Jones-Rounds et al., 2013)

These are not problems that a privileged 19-year-old with tarot cards can fix. These are certainly not issues best approached in a digital arena that celebrates wealth and serves to actually increase rather than reduce the sense of isolation and loneliness that people feel as a result of not having it. Social media is not the problem, but it is part of it, and I'm pretty sure it is, at best, a very small part of the solution. I also think a man in bed making fun of people showing off on the Internet can only hope to help a little bit.[3] Mental health challenges are societal problems that need societal solutions, but no one

Social media is not the problem, but it is part of it, and I'm pretty sure it is, at best, a very small part of the solution.

should be left on their own to find answers to the challenges that life presents, particularly if those challenges are made worse by difficult economic circumstances.

This does not mean that all the mental health advice on the Internet is bad advice. I'm sure that journalling *is* actually a good way to understand our thoughts and process them, but this process would definitely be better if the person advising us on the technique was available to speak to us about what we have written afterwards. Social media can often provide us with information, but can't then offer us support. For example, people online often prescribe getting outdoors into nature as a way to improve our mental health and, when this is an option, it is good advice, but it needs to be matched up with support to help people to do it.[4] This is where community – the subject of the Epilogue – is the final piece of the social media puzzle that can actually transform it from being isolating into a force for connection by empowering people.

We should talk about empowerment. I'm not sure I even know what it means, despite how widely it's used on social media. That might mean I am unempowered or maybe that the term has got blurred by wishy-washy usage and humblebrags. The main thing I notice is that most of the people I hear talking about empowerment are both (1) super-hot and (2) rich. Now, at any point in history, being rich and hot was pretty much the ultimate definition of already being empowered (mostly just the rich bit, to be honest, but being hot also meant you could slay in the portrait painted of you). So, if getting more money = getting

---

[3] Moi.
[4] Look online for groups, such as Black Girls Hike or The Hike Life, based in Ireland, both on Instagram.

more empowered, isn't it odd that none of the suggestions people offer online are things like 'campaign for a higher living wage' or 'join a union'. These are pretty classic empowerment tactics that have the extra benefit of helping other people who may be struggling. I firmly believe that they would achieve more if they did that than things like 'be unapologetically yourself'. Being yourself and not apologising for it are generally good things, but they are not going to help as many people as unapologetically demanding better working conditions or housing.

The problem is that actual empowerment is hard and takes a long time. Improving civil rights is an ongoing struggle that, to get where we are now, took centuries, marches and sometimes revolutions. These things don't fit into 30-second videos. So we end up with 'living your best life' as the solution, when, in reality, the best life you can live is shaped by the society you live in, laws and inequality. A hot girl summer cannot undo decades of cuts to social services. We cannot manifest our way to equality.

Manifesting is actually a big one online. So here's my take on it. Yes, it probably does work; no, it is probably not magic. Thinking about your goals positively and proactively probably does make them seem more achievable and become more achievable as a result. Manifesting without any action would obviously be completely pointless. I cannot manifest my way to becoming richer than Elon Musk or looking like David Gandy. If manifesting actually worked as well as people on the Internet say it does, then some of these experts would have manifested their way to a psychology degree or a therapy qualification, because there are a lot of people giving advice about our minds without any training.

Considering that there is a massive shortage of mental

health professionals in the UK, there is a real surplus of people talking about it online. According to the Royal College of Psychiatrists (2021), 1.5 mllion people are waiting for mental health treatment because there is a shortage of trained psychiatrists. Can we manifest some more into existence? No, but we could collectively demand that our government invests in training more mental health nurses, psychiatrists and therapists. There are clearly a lot of people with good intentions who want to help others by talking about mental health online, so it is down to people with power, real power, to do so to create the avenues for them to train and do so officially.

This is a sad truth about empowerment: anyone who can offer it to you in a short video is probably not in a position to provide it. They are more likely offering advice, or entertainment, when true empowerment requires structures to be built and far more substance than can fit on a Live, Laugh, Love cushion. We could live, laugh, love until the cows came home, but it wouldn't pay our rent, and it wouldn't even guarantee us a place any nicer than the one the cows came back to.

I also find the gender split in empowerment and mental health advice on social media quite odd. This happens across the Internet but, in this area, we seem to have ended up with quite a strong 'boys like blue and girls like pink' sort of approach. Male empowerment seems to me to be all about money, muscles and masculinity. This means that the manosphere is concerned with being tough, resilient and having an investment portfolio. And loathing women in many cases. It's not immediately clear why hating women should be part of an 'empowerment' project, but I think the Andrew Tates of this world genuinely see it as a subsection of an attempt to empower young men.[5] Live, lift, loathe, if you like. They are actually selling young men a particularly odious version of the 'live your best life' philosophy, in which this, they are told, requires that you subjugate others. I think this reflects badly on empowerment in general, even if we want to treat it as a separate issue. If empowerment is such a broad idea that it can be co-opted for the purposes of anyone who wants to access power, that means it can be used as a tool for terrible ends. When a lot of people feel disempowered (by society, by the economy, by the fast-changing world), people on the Internet can claim a great deal of poisonous power by offering them a solution.

From what I can see, the form of empowerment that gets marketed more to women (by very binary algorithms) appears less toxic and dangerous than the one being sold to men. It seems to usually involve floral prints and slogans but, in its own way, it is as much a simplification of the idea of empowerment as that which the manosphere offers (without the murderous rage). You need to be you.[6] Believe in yourself.[7] Live bravely.[8] Be soul-aligned.[9] While the manosphere assumes men are angry teenagers, the female empowerment sector treats women like children too. It assumes there is a crisis of bravery, that people are not themselves and the reason people are unhappy and fed up is because they haven't learnt to live their best life; when maybe they are just *angry* and fed up because they are having a bad time. The solution can't be that we all become life coaches.

----

[5] By 'empower', I mean make money from them.
[6] I am!
[7] I do! I'm real!
[8] OK! And do what?
[9] Huh?

The saddest thing about the binary portrayal of empowerment online is that the two communities might be better off swapping audiences (though, of course, this wouldn't solve the binary bit). Women[10] have a lot to be angry about, and could do with the sort of validation of their rage that the manosphere offers men. Many men could do with a bit more freedom to be sensitive. The dandelion headdresses would probably do a lot more good for the angry teenage boys than what they're getting from the manosphere at the moment. Yet we have a social media system that puts people in the boy box or the girl box and doesn't allow those in either box to draw from the advice given to those in the other box.

As a society, we have spent a long time breaking down the social norms around gender roles, but people on the Internet often seem set on reinstating them. This is supposed to be a modern platform, yet people on it seem so fixated on selling quite old-fashioned ideas. One side gets a Barbie version of empowerment, and the other Action Man. Well, I AM NOT A DOLL AND I AM ALSO NOT A CHILD, even if it feels like society sort of wants me to be one. A child, that is, not a doll.

I say that because the age bracket for the term 'young people' seems to have just extended off the charts in the last few years. Stories about there being a massive rise in the number of young people still living at home, with statistics of 1 in 4.5 households having adult children still living at home (Office for National Statistics, 2023), with the upper age limit for these young people and adult children being 35

---

[10] In both these cases, men and women, I am aware that I am making MASSIVE generalisations.

(Booth and Goodier, 2023). WHAT IS AN ADULT CHILD? I ask you kindly. I am not an adult child, I am a man who cannot afford to move out. Our society has moved the accepted age for 'young people' up towards 40 as a way of letting itself off the hook for massively failing to move income between generations.[11] If you tell someone that they are a 'young person' at 38, you can get away with making it impossible for them to buy a house or afford a family because they're just a pesky kid.

I mean, have you seen what 35-year-olds looked like in the 1950s and 1960s?[12] They were like 65-year-olds are now. They'd had the same job for 20 years, owned their home for 10 and had 5 kids. They didn't have a workplace that offered them beanbags and mini-basketball hoops, but they had a house. They didn't go to Ballie Ballerson ball pit cocktail bar on the weekends – they had grandchildren. I'm not saying being a wizened old 35-year-old with 20 years in the factory under your belt is necessarily better than what we have now, but it would be nice to have the option of certain aspects of adulthood. It would be nice not to have to accept children's party games as an alternative to the money, influence and social standing that previous generations could expect to develop in their 30s.[13]

Maybe this is one of the reasons for the mental health crisis? Maybe many of us are fed up with being treated like children by our society, so decide to act like it on the Internet. Maybe I should just have a cocktail and check out the ball

---

[11] Except in the case of inheritance, go figure.
[12] Martin Luther King Jr was 34 when he made his 'I have a dream' speech.
[13] Second shout-out to the excellent Blindboy podcast for his thoughts on this subject. Definitely check it out.

pit. I hear they have alcoholic slush puppies. You know, like the ones you had when you were a kid, but with vodka in them. Best of both worlds. But, ideally, we would actually have the best of both worlds. Adult ball pits/social mobility, table football in the office/a mortgage that was three times our salary, empowering slogans about 'being your truth'/ some sort of ability to collectively bargain for better living conditions. I don't know how we can get it, but maybe we can learn from some of our elders because we don't seem to really campaign very much any more.

Speaking to our elders is actually a good bit of povvo mental health advice. I'm not advocating for arranged marriages but speaking to a 93-year-old about her happy 70 years with a man she met on her wedding day is probably a handy way to put your arguments about who does the dishes into perspective. Old people are handy, free counsellors.[14]

Historically, societies have always looked up to their older people and, at times, this has been a bad thing, but I do wonder whether we have now gone too far the other way. I think the cult of youthful beauty has led to an absence of diversity in the advice we access. I cannot be a grown-ass adult taking advice from a 19-year-old who made his millions producing Minecraft raps. I need an aunty. We all need aunties. And uncles, but not so many of the uncles because they have had their time. Older people often have perspective, and they also have a good idea of how the world has changed and who effected that change. It is worth learning from them. We should ask gay rights campaigners from the 1980s how they got us to where we are today rather than arguing with

---

[14] But you do have to listen to them too. It's part of the deal. Unlike the Internet, these conversations go both ways.

incels on X. Find a second-wave feminist and ask how they managed to secure women's reproductive rights. Ask an older immigrant how they became happy in a new country that treated them so terribly. Ask all of them how they kept their head up when society's forces seemed intent on pressing them down. Because that advice *is* mental

> **❝ ❞**
>
> **I cannot be a grown-ass adult taking advice from a 19-year-old who made his millions producing Minecraft raps. I need an aunty.**

health advice but it is also a blueprint for changing those aspects of society that are making us unhappy. The income inequality, the lack of opportunity, the culture itself. That would be empowering and healthy.

I think it's time for some more tips. **Find a free community.** This might be in the form of volunteering somehow or doing something you like that doesn't cost money. Church choirs. Park runs. A group of litter heroes who clean up a local area or beach. Watching a man in his bed laugh at rich people. Whatever it is, if there is a sense of achievement and community, then it is a seriously good mental health practice.

Be politically conscious and active is another. Let's be honest, I couldn't go on about how the root causes of our mental health crisis and disempowerment were social and political without saying it. If you want society to be more equal, be vocal in your support for political movements that encourage it. Go canvassing, give out leaflets, do something that makes you feel like you are acting on the world rather than the world acting on you.

Free meditative practice. Yeah, I went there but, don't

worry, I'm not gonna sell you a guided meditation. Here, I mean the povvo kind. Like doing some knitting or sitting on your front porch on a hot day with your feet in a bucket and a napkin on your head. Read every part of the paper, from front to back. This is very closely related to the next one: **try not to give a damn.** Povvos, historically, were cast as uncouth, mouthy and opinionated, while keeping up appearances was for rich people. So, out of respect for that great tradition, say and feel what you want and try not to judge yourself. A povvo is loud and proud, and that is a great thing (though sleepy introverts are also welcome here). So what if you're not as beautiful or demure as someone on the Internet – you're probably happier for it.

This is very similar to **not hiding from your emotions.** Because bottling up emotions is a rich people habit. Our luxury is that we can express ourselves without fear of judgement, so get in the bath and have a loud cry. Go to the pub and have a loud cry. Have a loud cry and treat it as a political statement. It is an expression of your pride and your solidarity with your people.

Solidarity is a great thing and communities like ours have always had outlets for discussing our problems. So **rely on friends and family for helpful conversations.** I am not saying that we should avoid therapy or proper counselling if we are really struggling with our mental health because that is very important. What I mean is that, in cases where we are simply feeling low, have a worry or a problem, we are better off turning to someone who is a good listener than an Instagram wellness adviser.

A lot of people recommended **going for a walk**[15] and,

---

[15] Or however it is you move and/or get fresh air.

fair play, it's been the povvo solution to everything from transport costs to exercise, so why not put it up there as a positive mental health practice as well. I am gradually starting to believe that walking is basically the povvo elixir (after Vimto) – a solution for almost every situation. I should probably have called this book 'I'm rich, you're walking' because that seems to be what we're all up to and I love it. Being able to walk long distances is what helped our ancestors outcompete our ape cousins by moving on to the savannah, and it is clearly what is helping us povvos outcompete people with private jets and Bentleys. Some people recommended **loud, loud music** as a powerful modifier for this mental health practice, and I give that my seal of approval. Maybe sing along and cry as well. I've done it and can say without a doubt that it makes you feel better.

Tea is the one-word follow-up to the loud, long walk. So many people recommended it as a mental health practice and I am not one to question the hive mind. I wouldn't dare, and I would also be wrong if I did because we all know the restorative powers of the hot drink, particularly if you can share it with a good listener who has had their own share of problems to overcome. If you own a bath (you fancy dan), this will only increase the power of the tea.

All these tips are reminders that **self-care doesn't have to cost a lot.** Some people have recommended reality TV as a mental health practice, others Disney films. Just remember that whatever makes you happy and doesn't hurt anyone is a good thing in this world.

Consuming reality TV may also help you to action one of my favourite mental health recommendations, which I am going to quote directly as it was given to me on my Insta: **'I pretend I'm Karen Kardashian as I go to sleep at night'.**

Now I know this whole book has been about breaking out of the delusions of the social media age and being proud to be a povvo, but who hasn't enjoyed a little bit of healthy delusion at some time? I am going to go to sleep tonight imagining my escapades as Karen Kardashian, starting fights at a gender reveal party, getting drunk and running into the middle of an NBA game, removing all the labels from pantry items (THE HORROR). Basically, ruining the show. It sounds fun, even if you wouldn't want it to be your life all the time (Karen K is *a lot*), so it can remain as a bit of mental health escapism.

Being proud of yourself is a beautiful suggestion that came in from a lot of people. You know that your self-worth isn't tied to the money you have or the things you have bought, but you can be proud of every single thing you have achieved because none of it was given to you on a plate. If you are an ordinary person, struggling in a challenging world, you should be proud every day of your life for the fact that you are the one making it work. Imagine not being chuffed on the day you were able to buy your first dishwasher.[16] Rich people genuinely don't get that moment. If you inherit or can buy a big house with all the white goods, you never get that feeling of looking at a dishwasher and knowing you worked for it. You will never truly know how great and glorious a thing a dishwasher is as you've never been without one. As a povvo, you have far more space in your mind for gratitude and a far greater capacity to enjoy life's small wins than the rich. That is a good thing, and if you work at reminding yourself to be proud and keep enjoying those things that other people take for granted, you can consider yourself very lucky.

---

[16] This came up in my requests for povvo pride and it's perfect.

Considering yourself lucky is actually a deep and meaningful povvo principle because ignoring those who have less than us is a self-destructive luxury that only rich people can afford. We povvos don't see the people who have less than us as lazy or feckless. We know that the world can be a hard place if you are not born with privilege, and this leaves us more space in our hearts for empathy. If you are kind to others, you can be kind to yourself and this is a key tenet of good mental health. If you can do so with a sense that every act of kindness you put out into the world is an expression of community, you will be happier for it and maintain a tradition of generosity that povvos have maintained for millennia. I think one of the gang put it best when she said, 'Tipping even though I'm skint. I know we're all inthis together.'

If you are an ordinary person, struggling in a challenging world, you should be proud every day of your life for the fact that you are the one making it work.

Being 'in this together' is the most powerful thing we have. We may all feel like the odd ones out on the Internet because the people we are told to look at are beautiful, rich and isolated. But if we remind ourselves that there is nothing better than being normal, being part of a community, then we will know we have more than anyone who lives a seemingly perfect, isolated life.

This is the power of community. This is the povvogang.

BEG YOUR PAR
ROUND BALLY IC
RICH, YOU'RE PC
SPOKEN LIKE A
POVVO, BECAUS
NOT AN ANIMAL
WHY?, BECAUSE
YOU'RE A POVVC
WHAT ON GOD'S
EARTH, ON TODA
EPISODE OF..., RC
SISTER SHERRIE
HAVE A DAY OFF
GASP, STOP IT

EPILOGUE
COMMUNITY
AND POVVO
PRIDE

started making videos on social media because I often didn't know whether to laugh or cry at what I saw. I wanted to laugh because the celebrations of perfect lives and exclusivity were mostly ridiculous, and I wanted to cry because I knew how perfection and exclusivity could make people feel – imperfect and excluded.

I wasn't aware at the time but, while I made those videos, my followers were creating the only sort of space that could work as a response to such a problem, which was a community. It seems obvious now, but the best way to push back against a culture of exclusivity and individualism on the Internet is through inclusion and community. We had to create a sort of *anti* social media (ASMOs pending) where,

◀◀ ▶▶

The best way to push back against a culture of exclusivity and individualism on the Internet is through inclusion and community.

together, we celebrated our ordinariness and enjoyed the fact that there were lots of other people like us. Somehow, a community was imagined into existence, and we became part of it before we even realised we were one. I thought I was just making videos in my bed.

I should have seen it coming, though, because if there is one thing that povvos do well, it is build communities. Throughout history, we haven't had the right or the means to build walls or big houses around ourselves, so we have built our numbers and our networks. This still surprised me as it happened around *me*. I was surprised at the amount of pride the community had in being ordinary, which seems to be less normal now that people don't speak about class. I was surprised at how funny the comments were, and how they were more concerned with being witty than just criticising people in the videos. I was surprised at the level of agreement, which is odd because statements like, 'You probably don't need 10,000 perfumes' or 'paying $10,000 to eat dinner off another person's face is a bit odd'[1] are pretty hard to disagree with.

Yet I had never really heard people saying those things on the Internet before. I had always wondered if I was the only one who had noticed that social media could be kind of ridiculous. I started to think that there must just be something wrong with me, that I had some problem which meant I couldn't appreciate 'high-class face-based dining experiences' like everyone else. When, finally, I couldn't take it any longer and made a video (basically an external version of my internal monologue, which by that time was just my voice shouting 'WHY AM I BEING SHOWN RICH PEOPLE MAKING ICE ALL THE TIME?!'), things took off. I unloaded my frustration and tried to be funny and you all built a community around me. Then that community helped to write this book, because communities get things done.

So if that's true, what are we going to do, then? We're going to improve social media, and we're going to improve the world. With social media. Yes, you heard me right, we are going to make social media better through community and then use that community to have positive impacts on the outside world. These are my thoughts about how we could do it.

----

[1] I mean, you'll just have to look it up – it's on my page. There's an expensive restaurant where you pay $10,000 to eat food from a sort of plate that hangs off someone's face. Not much more I can say than that.

Starting with what I don't think. I don't think social media is necessarily bad. You see me there a lot, so it shouldn't come as a shock that I like it. I think it is still young and having some growing pains. I also don't think that being rich is absolutely bad. Inequality is bad, poverty is bad, and if we have to limit how rich some people can be to stop those bad things from happening, then I think we should. But I don't think it's a problem that people are rich. They can even film themselves if they like. People have a right to film their lives, they have a right to show off, and we have a right to laugh at it or ignore it. So we have to do that, more.

If we laugh at enough unrealistic stuff and ignore the rest, we can make social media better, because it is made of us. We have to use our humour and our intelligence, which is great because the community I have found online has those things in spades.

We need to start by choosing what we 'like' and what we celebrate carefully. Good things that empower people and make them happy should be championed and anything that does the opposite should be laughed at or ignored. When we have found those communities and people who contribute joy to the world, we need to amplify them online and then help translate that into good in the real world. Through this we can be active, rather than reactive, on social media before being proactive in the real world.

> **When we have found those communities and people who contribute joy to the world, we need to amplify them online and then help translate that into good in the real world.**

There are lots of examples of this. There are protest movements that started as hashtags and went on to change our public discourse and, later, our actual society. These are examples of the unifying power of social media – positive interpretations of platforms where millions of people can share an idea at once. That is a powerful thing. We discussed how it can be used to show off an expensive strawberry to a million people all at once, but it can also be a way to understand that you are a member of a group that is a million people strong. It can be a reminder of the strength we have in numbers, and this can help us feel empowered towards action.

So, first, let's look at some social media communities that have an impact on the real world locally, then we'll think about movements that try to have impacts on larger scales. I mentioned two in Chapter 10 that focus on hiking, so maybe we should home in on one of them. That community is Black Girls Hike. It started because Rhiane Fatinikun wanted to get into hiking, but couldn't find avenues for people from her background to get into the activity. So she started an Instagram page – not to show off how far she could walk or how good she looked in walking gear, but to tell more women like her that there was a community of people who would walk with them if they wanted to. She set up hikes and published the itineraries on social media channels. Instagram offered a way to communicate to a large group of people at once and, instead of using that lift herself, she used it to bring those people together. The Internet formed social bonds instead of distancing people. This is what I mean by the Internet being what we make it. More than five hundred people join these hikes now, and an activity that had seemed exclusive became inclusive through the Internet.

Another cool initiative is She Should Run in the USA. It's an Instagram page that encourages women to run for public office by raising awareness of the need for more public officials who are women and sharing resources that will help the next generation of women to run for these roles. They hold online seminars chaired by women who have succeeded in politics, offer advice on available positions to run for and use the network effects of social media to achieve the real-world political aim of more equal institutions.

We can also learn from the Pink Ladoo Project, which uses the Internet to celebrate the births of girls and reshape sexist norms, encouraging conversations about female children in South Asian communities. For many years in these communities, the birth of a girl has been a cause for disappointment rather than celebration, so the team behind Pink Ladoo decided to counter this by facilitating celebrations for girls through their pages and the resources they share. This is a way to use the Internet's strength in numbers to good effect.

It is also the literal opposite of sitting around feeling rubbish because someone is making really good ice. When our society is unequal and our online entertainment seems to celebrate that, we have to be strong enough to ignore or mock the bad entertainment and brave enough to engage with the structural problems that are creating them. Our community (povvogang) seems to be in agreement that society needs to be more equal. We want to laugh at rich people showing off, but I believe that we also want to do something about the fact so many of us are struggling. Political activism like She Should Run shows us one way to achieve this and Pink Ladoo another. They both lift people up through community, rather than press others down through individualism and false perfection.

We will probably have to do more than post AOC memes or point out on X that Conservative austerity policies in the UK have destroyed our public services. If people are going to be influencers, we should try to have some *actual* influence.[2] Social media can be entertaining and it can be useful, but it can also be a distraction, so we should try not to use it at the expense of doing things that have an impact in the real world. So if we're going to make changes, we should try to be a bit strategic about where and how we use our energy. This will be a personal choice, so I won't try to tell you what should matter to you, but I do want you to think about it. What is it that you wish you could change in the world? As an example, let's think about an issue of poverty, as it is related to the ideas in this book. Let's say that you want to stop children and their parents in your area from going hungry. You probably live in a developed economy, so this shouldn't be something that is happening. What can you do? You can support a food bank with your time, or a religious or community initiative that feeds people. You could publicise those initiatives on social media and ask people from your online communities to give their time too. This will help you to act on the issue locally. At a greater scale, you could think about how politics plays into the problem. Maybe your local MP represents a party or views that you think are contributing to the problem. You could research who the opposition party is and find out if they have a better alternative. If they do, then you could volunteer for them or distribute flyers in the run-up to an election.

---

[2] I've been called an 'anti-influencer', which is not strictly true. I'm all for people using the Internet to influence the world in positive ways. Who wouldn't be?

Better still, *you* could run for some kind of position and make the scandal of child poverty something you speak about every day.

You might think that sounds like a bit much, and if it is the case that you are completely overstretched and don't have time, then I understand. If you think it is a bit much because you wouldn't be capable or shouldn't be the sort of person making those decisions, then I disagree. Campaigners and changemakers have come from all walks of life, and the reason we only seem to end up with privately educated snobs in charge of our country is because they are the only people who are told they have a right to be in charge. If never doubting yourself is a condition for having influence, we will never have normal people making the decisions. Normal people doubt themselves, but normal people need to be involved.

> **If never doubting yourself is a condition for having influence, we will never have normal people making the decisions.**

Maybe you want to go bigger. Maybe you want to go global. We have seen how the climate justice movement has proudly taken up a lot of public space and airtime in the past few years, because people like Greta Thunberg and activists all over the globe have been willing to go outside and speak up. If you agree with climate protests, if you are concerned about climate change, be confident enough to shout about it. Protests are community events that make us feel good and achieve things. Communities get things done.

I realise that I am getting above my station, acting like a union organiser, but we all have to be shameless. We can't let all the shamelessness be reserved for rich influencers and rich politicians. Shame is a powerful force that only seems to be reserved for ordinary people. Rich people don't have to feel shame. So shame on them for making us feel like we need to keep quiet. Shame on them for making us feel ashamed of having less. But shame on us if we feel too ashamed to speak out and act up in favour of some changes.

I started making videos because I didn't know whether to laugh or cry at the state of social media. Then you created a community around those videos that went on to write this book. Now this book is finished, I feel more certain than ever that our community can achieve even more. We can make change. We can demand it.

Who would have thought that people making ice on social media could start something so beautiful?

Who would have thought that we could create a community out of it?

Who even reads *epilogues*?

You do, you beautiful povvos. Because you're getting your money's worth.

Now go and get even more of what you deserve.

Yours, Ibegyourpardonly,
Shabaz Ali (ShabazSays)

BEG YOUR PAR
ROUND BALLY IC
RICH, YOU'RE PO
SPOKEN LIKE A
POVVO, BECAUS
NOT AN ANIMAL
WHY?, BECAUSE
YOU'RE A POVVO
WHAT ON GOD'S
EARTH, ON TODA
EPISODE OF..., RO
SISTER SHERRIE
HAVE A DAY OFF
GASP, STOP IT

BIBLIOGRAPHY

@asahdkhaled (2021) 'Asahd's 5th birthday', Instagram. Available at: www.instagram.com/p/CVatSCKA2Sa/?hl=en (accessed October 2023).

The Apprentice (UK), (2021) 'Most INAPPROPRIATE branding in The Apprentice history', *The Apprentice* (UK), YouTube. Available at: www.youtube.com/watch?v=EQ8K-DlNeMk&ab_channel=TheApprenticeUK (accessed October 2023).

Bonner, Mehera (2023) 'Kim Kardashian installed pink carpeting for Chicago's birthday and Twitter is spiraling', *Cosmopolitan*, 26 January. Available at: www.cosmopolitan.com/entertainment/celebs/a42669233/kim-kardashian-pink-carpet-chicago-party-tweets/_ (accessed October 2023).

Booth, Robert (2023) 'Hunt and Braverman among five in Cabinet earning thousands as landlords', *The Guardian*, 4 May. Available at: www.theguardian.com/politics/2023/may/04/hunt-and-braverman-among-five-in-cabinet-earning-thousands-as-landlords (accessed October 2023).

Booth, Robert and Goodier, Michael (2023) 'Number of adults living with parents in England and Wales rises by 700,000 in a decade', *The Guardian*, 10 May. Available at: www.theguardian.com/society/2023/may/10/number-adults-living-parents-england-wales-up-700000-decade (accessed October 2023).

Bowenbank, Starr (2023) 'Watch Blue Ivy's dance skills evolve during Renaissance world tour in TikTok', *Billboard*, 29 September. Available at: www.billboard.com/music/music-news/blue-ivys-dance-skills-evolve-renaissance-world-tour-tiktok-1235429458 (accessed October 2023).

Burberry (2022) 'Burberry x Blankos Block Party: New NFT collection and social space', Burberry's website, 20 June. Available at: www.burberryplc.com/news/brand/2022/burberry-x-blankos-block-party--new-nft-collection-and-social-sp (accessed October 2023).

Hague, Molly-Mae (2022) 'Beyoncé has the same 24 hours in the day that we do', DailymotionNationalWorld.com, YouTube. Available at: www.dailymotion.com/video/x86xby6 (accessed October 2023).

Jones, Amy (2023) 'Inside Khloé Kardashian's elaborate first day at school for daughter True', *OK!*, 30 August. Available at: www.ok.co.uk/lifestyle/gallery/inside-khloe-kardashians-elaborate-first-30818846 (accessed October 2023).

Maguire, Lucy (2022) 'TikTock unboxing: Luxury fashion's low-cost marketing tool', *Vogue*, 2 September. Available at: www.voguebusiness.com/fashion/tiktok-unboxing-luxury-fashions-low-cost-marketing-tool (accessed October 2023).

Mental Health Foundation (n.d.) 'Poverty: statistics', Mental Health Foundation's website. Available at: www.mentalhealth.org.uk/ explore-mental-health/statistics/poverty-statistics (accessed October 2023). Sources of statistics, in order quoted: Gutman, L. M, Joshi, H., Parsonage, M. and Schoon, I. (2015) 'Children of the new century: Mental health findings from the Millennium Cohort Study' (London: Centre for Mental Health); Stansfeld, S., Clark, C., Bebbington, P., King, M., Jenkins, R. and Hinchliffe, S. (2016) 'Common mental disorders', in S. McManus, P. Bebbington, R. Jenkins and T. Brugha (eds), Mental health and wellbeing in England: Adult Psychiatric Morbidity Survey 2014 (Leeds: NHS Digital), Chapter 2; Jones-Rounds, M. L., Evans, G. W. and Braubach, M. (2013) 'The interactive effects of housing and neighbourhood quality on psychological well-being', *Journal of Epidemiology and Community Health*, 68(2): 171–175.

Office for National Statistics (2023) 'More adults living with their parents', Office for National Statistics' website. Available at: www.ons.gov.uk/peoplepopulationand community/ populationandmigration/populationestimates/articles/ moreadultslivingwith theirparents/2023-05-10#:~:text =In%20 2021%2C%20around%201%20in,4.9%20million%20in%20 Census%202021 (accessed October 2023).

Osifo, Ehis (2021) 'Apparently, Yolanda wouldn't buy Bella a pair of Louboutins in high school, which she said had a negative impact on her growing up', BuzzFeed, 17 November. Available at: www.buzzfeed.com/ehisosifo1/bella-hadid-didnt-wear-designer-in-high-school (accessed October 2023).

Petter, Olivia (2019) 'Barbra Steisand reveals she cloned dog because she "couldn't bear to lose her"', *Independent*, 22 March. Available at: www.independent.co.uk/life-style/barbra-streisand-clone-dog-the-times-brexit-a8835726.html (accessed October 2023).

Pickett, Kate and Wilkinson, Richard (2010) *The Spirit Level: Why equality is better for everyone* (London: Penguin).
Prendergast, Kelly (2023) 'Merchandizing the void', *Dilettante Army*, Spring. Available at: https://dilettantearmy.com/articles/merchandizing-the-void (accessed October 2023).

Rein, Lia (2017) 'I am very smart', *The Apprentice* (UK), YouTube. Available at: www.youtube.com/watch?v=JWFs Ue88gow&ab_channel=LiaRein (accessed October 2023).

Royal College of Psychiatrists (2021) 'Workforce shortages in
    mental health cause "painfully" long waits for treatment', Press
    release, Royal College of Psychiatrists' website, 6 October.
    Available at: www.rcpsych.ac.uk/news-and-features/latest-
    news/detail/2021/10/06/workforce-shortages-in-mental-health-
    cause-painfully-long-waits-for-treatment#:~:text=Record%20
    numbers%20of%20people%20need,of%205%2C317)%20are%20
    not%20filled (accessed October 2023).

Spillane, James (2023) 'Social media strategy: Rebranding
    heritabea t Burberry', Business @ Community, 12 May.
    Available at: www.business2community.com/social-media-
    articles/social-media-strategy-rebranding-heritage-at-
    burberry-02138561 (accessed October 2023).

Walton, Adele (2020) 'The dark truth about Dubai's influencer
    marketing', *Tribune*, 4 December. Available at: https://
    tribunemag.co.uk/2020/12/the-dark-truth-about-dubais-
    influencer-marketing (accessed October 2023).

Weather Maker (2015) 'The infamous interviews: This The
    Apprentice's greatest ever moment has to be Poor...',
    Weather Maker, YouTube. Available at: www.youtube.com/
    watch?v=7_9IlYOgSLQ&ab_channel=WeatherMaker
    (accessed October 2023).

BEG YOUR PARI
ROUND BALLY IC
RICH, YOU'RE PO
SPOKEN LIKE A
POVVO, BECAUS
NOT AN ANIMAL
WHY?, BECAUSE
YOU'RE A POVVO
WHAT ON GOD'S
EARTH, ON TODA
EPISODE OF..., RC
SISTER SHERRIE
HAVE A DAY OFF
GASP, STOP IT

ACKNOWLEDGEMENTS

Thank you to my parents, for always teaching me to be kind, even when faced with unkindness, and for letting me be myself, but, most importantly, always trusting in me.

Thanks also to my niece, Zoya, who lights up my life and makes me smile every single day.

To Sophie and Sabeeqa, for being my rocks, putting up with all the tears and tantrums, always keeping me humble and believing in me when I don't always believe in myself.

To Nora, Carly and Naomi at TMA, who have my back, work hard every day to help me make my dreams a reality and always push me to achieve greatness.

To Oscar, my co-writer, for understanding my vision and writing so brilliantly. You truly are a master wordsmith. Thank you for helping make this book everything I wanted it to be.

To all my friends and family, who have supported me over the years and who never stopped believing in me.

To Elizabeth and the team at DK, for making all this possible and believing in me and my book.

And to the povvogang, for providing some of the best material for this book!